Activity Assemblies for Christian Collective Worship 5–11

Anyway!

People are unreasonable, illogical and self centred.
Love them anyway!
If you do good, people will accuse you of selfish
    ulterior motives.
Do good anyway!
If you are successful, you will win false friends
    and true enemies!
Succeed anyway!
Honesty and frankness make you vulnerable.
Be honest and frank anyway!
The good you do today will be forgotten tomorrow.
Do good anyway!
The biggest people with the biggest ideas can be
    shot down by the smallest people with the
    smallest minds.
Think big anyway!
People favour underdogs but follow topdogs.
Fight for some underdogs anyway!
What you spent years building may be destroyed
    overnight.
Build anyway!
Give the world the best you have and you'll
    get kicked in the teeth.
Give the world the best you've got anyway!

Activity Assemblies for Christian Collective Worship 5–11

Elizabeth Peirce

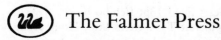 The Falmer Press

(A member of the Taylor & Francis Group)
London ● New York ● Philadelphia

UK   The Falmer Press, Rankine Road, Basingstoke, Hampshire, RG24 0PR

USA   The Falmer Press, Taylor & Francis Inc., 1900 Frost Road, Suite 101, Bristol, PA 19007

© E.C. Peirce 1991

First published in 1991

British Library Cataloguing in Publication Data

Peirce, Elizabeth
Activity assemblies for Christian collective worship, 5–11.
1. Primary schools. Morning assembly
I. Title
377.14
ISBN 1-85000-728-4

Library of Congress Cataloging-in-Publication Data
Peirce, Elizabeth.
Activity assemblies for Christian collective worship, 5–11/ Elizabeth Peirce.
p.   cm.
Includes bibliographical references
ISBN 1-85000-728-4: — ISBN 1-85000-729-2 (pbk.):
1. Worship (Religious education) 2. Religion in the public schools — Great Britain. I. Title.
BV26.P45 1991
377'.14 — dc20   90-41516
                                                CIP

Jacket design and illustrations by Benedict Evans

Jacket drawing by Antonia Bolton

Typeset in 11/13pt Bembo by
Graphicraft Typesetters Ltd., Hong Kong.

Printed and bound in Great Britain by Taylor & Francis (Printers) Ltd. Basingstoke

Contents

Dedication

To Di Dobson and the East Sussex Schools' Library Service without whose help this book could not have been produced; to Fiona Shore, BBC Producer Schools Radio and Editor of *Hands Together*, whose confidence in me first inspired me to write down my ideas; to the children and teachers of East Sussex who were my guinea-pigs; to my mother who encouraged me to put it all together; and to my husband who gave me many ideas.

Acknowledgments

'Friends and Neighbours'. The discussion was first published by E.C. Peirce as 'People and Relationships' in the BBC teachers' notes for the radio programme *Discovery*, 1987.

The discussion and follow-up activities for the 'Losing Friends Assembly' were first published by E.C. Peirce as 'How Would You Feel If . . .' in the BBC teachers' notes for the radio programme *Discovery*, 1987.

'People Who Help Us' discussion and 'People Who Need Help' discussion were first published by E.C. Peirce in the BBC teachers' notes for the radio programme *Discovery, 1987.*

'The Chess Game' (adapted for radio by E.C. Peirce) was first broadcast on 26 November 1987 as part of the BBC children's radio education programme *Discovery*. It was based on R. Brandling, *The Chess Match, Assembly Poems & Prose* (Macmillan, 1977).

'Easter: The Ugly Man' (adapted for radio by E.C. Peirce) was first broadcast on 15 October 1987 as part of the BBC children's radio education programme *Discovery*. It was based on D. Moss. He Died for US, *Today's Talks for Today's Children* (Chester House Publications, 1967).

'Giving and Sharing' was first published by E.C. Peirce in the Scholastic Magazine, *Hands Together*, 5, July 1984. It was first broadcast on 3 December 1987 as part of the BBC children's radio education programme *Discovery*. The notes and activities for *Giving and Sharing* were first published as the 'Wider World' in the BBC teachers' notes for the radio programme *Discovery*.

The discussion and follow-up activities for 'Our Senses: Eyes' and 'Our Senses: Ears' were first published by E.C. Peirce in the BBC teachers' notes for the radio programme *Discovery*, 1987.

'Heroes and Heroines: Bravery and Courage' was first published by E.C. Peirce as 'What Makes People Brave' in the BBC teachers' notes for the radio programme *Discovery*, 1987.

Background information on Christianity was first published by E.C. Peirce as part of the teachers' notes for the BBC radio programme *Contact*, 1988.

'A Pageant', 'Dress up a Child', 'A Dustman Dance', 'A Story of an Ordinary Man Who Helped Others' were first published in the Scholastic Magazine *Hands Together*, 4 May 1984.

'True Love' (adapted by E.C. Peirce) was first published in the Scholastic Magazine *Hands Together*, 5 July 1984. It was based on O. Henry, *The Gift of the Magi*.

'From a Seed to a Chair', 'A Loaf of Bread', 'Sharing Our Harvest Gifts: A Bowl of Rice', 'Preserving Our Harvest Gifts: A Tin of Fish', 'A Harvest Tea at School', 'Harvest of Ourselves' were first published by E.C. Peirce in the Scholastic Magazine *Hands Together*, 6 September 1984.

'Sunrise', 'New Year Celebrations', 'First Day at School', 'Baptism', 'Celebration of New Life after Death' were first published by E.C. Peirce in the Scholastic Magazine *Hands Together*, 8 January 1985.

'People Who Use the Church', 'A Closer Look inside and outside a Church', 'Interview a Vicar', 'St Margaret', 'Elijah's Story' were first published by E.C. Peirce in the Scholastic Magazine *Hands Together*, 10 May 1985.

'The Good Me and the Bad Me', 'Study of a Neighbourhood', 'Losing Friends', 'The Lion and the Mouse', 'The Case for Team Spirit', 'Choosing Friends Assembly: Rogues' Gallery' were first by published by E.C. Peirce in the Scholastic Magazine *Hands Together*, 11 July, 1985.

'St George, St Patrick, St Andrew and St David', 'Gideon', 'Sybil Phoenix: A Modern-day Saint', 'St Francis of Assisi', 'St Paul' were first published by E.C. Peirce in the Scholastic Magazine *Hands Together*, 16 May 1986.

'Water Projects', 'Lack of Water', 'Clean and Dirty', 'The Man Who Took Seven Baths', 'A Rain Dance', 'Calming of the Storm'. 'A "Thank You" Book about Water' were first published by E.C. Peirce in the Scholastic Magazine *Hands Together*, 17 July 1986.

'A Sleepy Dance for Hibernating Animals', 'Harvest of the Hedgerows', 'Pin the Load on the Donkey', 'The Lost Sheep', 'The Good Shepherd', 'Miracle of Migration', 'Animals and Insects Giving for Our Harvest' were first published by E.C. Peirce in the Scholastic Magazine *Hands Together*, 18 September 1986.

'Exploring a Typical English Church' (E.C. Peirce December 1986), 'The Twelve Days of Christmas' (E.C. Peirce December 1987) and 'Noah's Ark' (E.C. Peirce, June 1988) were first published in the Scholastic Magazine *Child Education*.

'Moving House' was adapted from the story by D. Moss, 'Love Is a Runner Bean' in *Today's Talks for Today's Children*. (Chester House Publications, 1967).

'Colours: Saints, Signs & Symbols' illustrations & quotations are reproduced by kind permission of S.P.C.K., W. Ellwood Post, *Saints, Signs & Symbols* © 1962, 1974, Morehouse Barlow Co.

'Choosing Friends Assembly: Rogues Gallery', the drama activity is based on an idea by R. Wood in *Activity Talks with Boys and Girls*, N.C.E.C., 1972.

'The Parable of the Good Punk Rocker' and 'The Unforgiving Servant', are reproduced from P. Burbridge and M. Watts *Time to Act* (Hodder and Stoughton Limited, 1979).

'A Loaf of Bread' was an idea given to the author by Rev. Jennings, Methodist minister, Eastbourne.

'A Bowl of Rice' was adapted from a lesson in the RE Handbook: *A Resource for Primary School Teachers*, Ed. Margaret Ashby (Scripture Union, 1983) by permission of Scripture Union.

'The Rain' and 'The Song of the Waves' are reproduced from *Poems for Movement*, edited by E.J.M. Woodland London (Evans, 1966).

The idea of using happy and sad masks for 'The Lost Sheep' is reproduced by kind permission and was from J. Gattis Smith, *Show Me* Creative Resources 2 (Bible Society, 1985).

'Psalm 23' and most of the other biblical references are from the *Good News Bible*, published by Bible Society/Collins and reproduced with the permission of the publishers. (Some references, where stated, are from the *Revised Standardized Version* of the Bible.)

'Sybil Phoenix' is based on an account by John Newbury in *Living in Harmony* (Religious & Moral Education Press, 1985).

'The Unknown Boy Hero' was adapted for the BBC radio programme *Discovery*, 1987 by E.C. Peirce from the story, 'People Aren't Always What They Seem', in R.H. Lloyd, *Assemblies for School and Children's Church* (Religious & Moral Education Press, 1974). It was first broadcast on 8 October 1987.

'Pentecost or Whitsunday Assembly' was based on an idea given to the author by Rev. R. Mann, Broadwell, Gloucester.

'Hide and Seek', and 'Sleepy Baby', from D. Evans, *Fingers, Feet and Fun!* (Beaver Ed., 1986) are reproduced by kind permission of Random Century Limited.

'An Ordinary Day' by Norman MacCaig is reproduced by kind permission of the author.

'Bravery' by A. Farncombe is reproduced by kind permission of NCEC.

Every effort has been made to trace the owners of all copyright material. In one or two cases this has proved impossible. The author will be pleased to correct any omissions in future editions and give full acknowledgments.

Hymn Books

Apusskidu, A. and C. Black, 1975.
Carol, Gaily Carol, A. and C. Black, 1973.
Child Songs, Pilgrim Press, Reprint 1959.
Come and Praise, BBC Reprint, 1985.
Come and Sing, Scripture Union, 1971.
Count Me In, A. and C. Black, 1984.
Every Colour Under the Sun, Ward Lock, 1983.
Game-Songs with Prof Dogg's Troupe, A. and C. Black, 1983.
Infant Praise, Oxford University Press, 1964.
Mango Spice, A. and C. Black, 1981.
New Child Songs, Denholm House Press, 1973.
New Life, Galliard, 1971.

Acknowledgments

Sing a Song of Celebration, Holt Rinehart and Winston, 1984.
Sing it in the Morning, Nelson, 1975.
Someone's Singing Lord, A. and C. Black, 1973.
Songs of Fellowship, Kingsway Publications Limited, 1979.
Tinder-box: 66 Songs for Children, A. and C. Black, 1982.

Introduction

Preparing an assembly every day of the week, each week of the term, year in and year out, is one of the most demanding tasks for headteachers and class teachers alike, (Education Reform Act 1988, section 6: 7). To begin with, one has to pitch what one says to an audience that varies not only in age and understanding but also in culture and religious belief. It is a task that is almost too daunting to contemplate, yet faced with the reality of a hall full of children, one has to provide something that draws everyone together, so that all children feel a sense of belonging, a sense of community, a sense of being part of a caring, sharing group with the common title of 'Our School.'

In order to use the ideas in this book, much will depend on the physical conditions and numerical arrangements of children in individual schools. For instance, an important factor will be whether teachers take separate assemblies for Infant and Juniors, or whether assemblies are taken all together. With this in mind, age ranges have been indicated, but it may be necessary to adapt teaching styles and techniques to suit older or younger children, or indeed to suit the whole primary range taken together.

In addition, the needs of the small rural primary school will vary enormously, from the needs of the large inner city school, and teachers will have to use their professional judgement to assess appropriateness, in selecting material. Projects are not inter-dependent, and so can be selected at random, to reinforce topic work being followed in school.

Hall space too, will be a major consideration. It may be, that for some, much of the activity will have to take place in the confines of the classroom, where hall space is limited or non-existent. It is intended that assemblies will form an integral part of the whole of school life. Therefore themes and projects have been provided that cover a great deal of curricular activity, culminating in an assembly. Children learn best from concrete experience, from which abstract ideas will gradually be understood. Therefore, much of the material presented, is intended to be experiential, starting from where the child is, and moving on to widen horizons and to extend experiences, by taking children out on visits, or inviting visitors into school. In addition, assemblies covering the main Christian Festivals, Saints Days and Rites of Passage have been included.

Perhaps it is important to remember, that an activity assembly every day is not always the answer, since one is reduced to trying to 'better' one 'performance' with the next. But a quiet reflective story interspersed with an activity assembly, caters for the different moods and needs of the school. For instance, after an exciting event in school, it is far better to have a quiet story; but if the children are quiet, a dramatic assembly such as the story of 'Elijah' in part 12, has the effect of making everyone sit up and participate.

Finally, the Education Reform Act states, that the act of worship should 'reflect the broad traditions of Christian belief without being distinctive of any particular denomination,' (Education Reform Act 1988, section 7: 2). Even as a Christian myself, I believe that leading children into a particular faith is the task of the home. Educating children is the school's task. This book is the first in a two volume series. The second book deals with multi-cultural and multi-racial activities. It is hoped that these two books together, can be used across the faiths, as, they are not distinctive of any particular faith, but rather child-centred. The school should create an atmosphere where belief in God can grow. It is part of our spiritual development that makes us into complete people. It is this 'holistic' approach to education, the development of a sense of awe and wonder, the positive attitude to life and learning, the awareness of the needs and gifts of others, that I want the children to learn. I hope that nothing offends any particular religious group, but rather creates a better understanding of each other's beliefs. After all, parents still have the final sanction, of their children's non-participation in school assembly, but if this should happen, then much of the community feeling, the ethos of the school, will be lost forever, and today's children will grow up holding on to many of the deep prejudices that divide our world today.

1   New Beginnings

5–11
Assembly

Myself

The aim of this assembly is to introduce ourselves to one another. It could be spread over several days, beginning with the school staff, i.e. the teachers, the headteacher, the caretaker and cleaners, cooks, dinner helpers, school crossing patrol person, First-Aid person, secretary, etc.

Just a brief word from each person saying who they are and what they do is needed, and a simple prayer of thanks for their contribution to school life at the end of the assembly, will help the children to appreciate the different roles.

A class of children could develop this theme by doing a project on Myself: Who am I? Include the following points: hair colour, weight, eye colour, height, my mother or father or family; I am a boy or girl; I can shout, laugh, cry, smile; I can jump, skip, swim; food I like, the time I go to bed, etc.; I am unique.

At the beginning of the school year it is fun to weigh each child in each class and then add all the weights together for the whole school. Then do the same thing at the end of the school year and compare the weights. It is great fun to compare the additional weight gained by the children (and staff) at the end of the year with the weight, say, of an elephant at London Zoo!

Prayer

Thank you God, for making me, me. Thank you for my special gifts and talents, for my ability to laugh and sing and shout and play. Help me to make my own proper contribution to school life. Amen.

Hymn

No. 19 'He gave me eyes so I could see' in *Someone's Singing Lord* (A. and C. Black) or No. 73, 'Glad that I live am I' in *New Life* (Galliard).

Additional material

This poem can be used with children 5–7:
'Hide and Seek' from D. Evans *Fingers, Feet and Fun* (Beaver Ed., 1986)
(reproduced here by kind permission of Random Century Limited).

> I play hide and seek with me.
> I wonder wherever I can be?
> I look at the chair.
> No, I'm not there.
> I look at the mat.
> No, that's the cat.
> I wonder wherever I can be?
> I look in the mirror and I find me!

5–7
Assembly

Babies

Invite a mother and her baby into school. Explain to the children that this assembly is going to be a celebration of new life. Many young children will have had to come to terms with a new baby at home and may need help in coping with feelings of jealousy and rejection. We need to transmit something of the joy, fun and great interest that a new baby can bring.

Preparation for the Mother

If the mother is willing, explain that one of your aims is to make siblings feel loved and wanted, and so ask the mother if she will tell the children this, while chatting about the new baby at home. Perhaps she could bring in some baby clothes, or bath the baby for the children in the assembly and talk about all the equipment that is needed for bathing, dressing, feeding, etc.

Preparation for the Children in School

Perhaps the top infant children could prepare a list of questions to ask the mother from the floor:

1 What is the baby's name?
2 How old is he?
3 How much did the baby weigh at birth?
4 How much does the baby weigh now?
5 How many times a day is the baby fed?
6 What is he fed on?
7 What sort of noise does he make when he is happy? sad? angry?
8 What time does he go to bed?
9 What time does he get up?
10 How many times a day does he have his nappy changed?
11 What happens when he goes to the clinic?
12 How many times do you bath him a week?
13 How do you get the water to the right temperature?

14 What sort of games do you play with him?
15 What sort of toys does he have?

Allow sufficient time for questions and answers. Then thank the mother and baby for coming into school. Explain that the children will say a special prayer of thanks for this wonderful new life and for the well-being of mum, and then the children can sing a quiet hymn.

Prayer

Heavenly Father, We do thank you that Mrs ... [name] was able to visit us today and bring in baby ... [name]. We have so enjoyed their visit and have learnt so much about new babies. We know that you love each one of us just as much as you love this new baby. Thank you for the gift of new life and we ask you to bless ... [name] and all the family. Amen.

Hymn

No. 36, 'We will take care of you' in *Every Colour Under the Sun* (Ward Lock Educational); or No. 3, 'Morning has broken' in *Someone's Singing Lord* (A. and C. Black).

Poem

Suitable for 5 year olds: 'Sleepy Baby' from D. Evans *Fingers, Feet and Fun* (Beaver Ed., 1986) (reproduced here by permission of Random Century Limited).

Sleepy Baby

I am a baby fast asleep.
  Eyes closed, head resting on hands.
I open my eyes to take a peep.
  Open eyes.
I lift up my head to look around.
  Lift head and look around.
I open my mouth — make a yawning sound.
  Yawn.
I lift up my arms and stretch up high.
  Stretch.

I think I might be going to cry.
Arms down, sad face.
Oh no, I won't, I'll go back to sleep.
Head resting on hands again.
I'll close my eyes and not even peep!
Close eyes and be very still.

Moving House

(Adapted from the story 'Love is a runner bean' in D. Moss *Today's Talks for Today's Children* (Chester House Publications, 1967).)

This story could be mimed while it is being told.

Two friends, John and Mary, lived next door to each other in a tall block of flats in a huge city. Soon they were going to move to a new housing estate and each would have a small garden. They were both delighted because they had never had a garden before. Everything had to be packed up and put into big boxes and there was a lot of rubbish that had to be thrown away.

Soon the great day for removal arrived and the children couldn't contain their excitement. They were looking forward to moving into their new homes and to going to their new school and to making new friends. They were especially looking forward to having a garden of their own. The men loaded all the furniture onto the van and helped the two families move into their new houses on the same estate. The children were not next door to each other this time, but they were only a few doors away from each other.

Although it was a bit strange at first, as soon as the children's own special things were unpacked, the houses began to feel more like homes and the children's parents told the children that they could each have a very small patch in their new gardens to grow their very own vegetables or flowers.

After a great deal of thought, the children decided to grow runner beans. They worked very hard in their own gardens, first digging the soil [mime the action], then planting the beans and finally planting firm canes into the ground to support the beans as they grew. Each day the children watered the seeds and kept their garden patch free from weeds and soon the bean plants began to grow and twist around the poles and produce little tiny beans.

As soon as John's beans were as big as his little finger, he picked them and gave them to his Mum to cook for the family's Sunday lunch. It was a very special occasion and there were just enough beans to give each person in John's family a tiny portion to taste. They were delicious.

Mary, on the other hand, decided not to pick her beans or to share them with anyone. She told her Mum that she wanted to let them grow until they were the biggest and fattest in the whole neighbourhood and then eat them all by herself as she had grown them.

In the meantime a very strange thing happened. Every time John picked his small green beans, more and more appeared. So he gave some to his new neighbours and to an old lady who lived on her own down the street, and he took some to his new teacher and to the lollipop lady at school and still more beans grew and grew.

Mary's beans, however, continued to grow very long and fat. No *new* beans appeared on her plants. The original beans just grew longer and fatter. Indeed, they were the biggest beans in the whole neighbourhood.

The great day came, when Mary decided to pick her beans and have them for Sunday lunch. But they were so tough and stringy that no one in her family could eat them. So they were left politely on the side of the plate. Mary burst into tears. Why were her beans so tough and inedible, when she knew that lots of people had greatly enjoyed eating John's beans?

Her mother explained. The more you pick runner beans, the more you get. They just keep on growing. But if you leave them, they grow very long and tough. She told Mary that this was a bit like being friendly. The more you give friendship to others, the more you get back. John lovingly gave all his beans away to feed his new neighbours and his plants produced many beans. But Mary kept all her beans to herself and as a result the beans became old and tough and stringy.

John made lots of new friends and settled very quickly and happily into his new home and school. But Mary felt lonely and unhappy and wanted to return to the big city.

Prayer

Heavenly Father, We sometimes find it difficult when we move house and leave old friends and familiar places behind. Help us to make new friends by being loving and friendly and generous to others. Amen.

Hymn

No. 42, 'Seeds of kindness', in *Every Colour under the Sun* (Ward Lock Educational); or No. 51, 'I've just moved into a new house', in *Tinder-box 66 Songs for Children* (A. and C. Black).

First Day at School

Ask the children to write about all that they remember of their first day at school. Allow the children to read their work to the rest of the school. The teacher could comment as necessary. The work could be accompanied by children's paintings depicting some of the most important aspects of school life — their new friends, their new teachers, what they do at school, etc.

The older children should then be encouraged to help all the new children to settle in as quickly and as happily as possible. Perhaps the older children could each befriend a new child and help him/her throughout the week, especially at play times and at dinner times and show him/her the daily routine.

This could be followed by the older children dramatizing an incident about including and rejecting friends in movement and mime. To do this, a group of children should mime playing happily together — 'Ring a Ring o' Roses', or 'In and out the Dusky Bluebells'. One child is left out — an outsider, a new child. She makes several attempts to join the group, to link hands with the other children. As she does this, every child in the group stops playing and puts both hands up in a threatening and forbidding gesture and simultaneously the group turn their heads away from the outsider. The children freeze in this position for one or two seconds, and then the child tries to join the group once more, only to be rebuffed in a similar way.

Eventually the lonely child turns away from the group and goes and sits on her own with her head in her hands and quietly weeps. At this point the teacher should explain that she does not want anyone in her school to feel as lonely and as left out as this child and that all the children in the school must make a real effort to make new children feel welcome, especially on their first day.

The mime is then performed again and this time the new child is made to feel welcome and loved.

Prayer

Heavenly Father, Help us to make our schools warm and welcoming places where everyone feels that they belong and everyone has a friend.

Hymn

No. 31, 'Thank you for my friends' in *Tinder-box 66 Songs for Children* (A. and C. Black).

New Year Celebrations

Begin with a child dressed up as an old man walking slowly across the front of the hall. In one hand he carries a stick; in the other hand he lifts a lantern to light his way.

A little boy stops him and says, 'Old man, give me your lantern, so that I can see clearly into the New Year.'

The old man replies, 'No. Go out into the darkness and put your hand into the hand of God. That will be much better than my light and much safer than any other way' (M. Louise Haskins).

The theme of New Year celebrations could be spread over the first few weeks of the new term.

Diwali, the Hindu festival of lights, does not coincide with our own New Year but provides a marvellous starting point for New Year celebrations. Diva (special lights) could be placed all around the hall. The story of Rama and Sita could be retold in dramatic form. The second volume in this series has more ideas for assemblies on the topic of Diwali.

The Chinese New Year can also provide a stimulating and colourful starting point for further investigation. This falls on a day between the middle of January and the middle of February. Parcels of sweets and money are wrapped in red paper; everyone puts on their best clothes and visits friends and relations; there are games and fireworks. It is the time when the popular Lion Dance is performed. Perhaps a group of children could make a Chinese lion mask and dance their version of this traditional activity. Read the Chinese New Year story in the Tinder-box Assembly book.

Other New Year celebrations could include a traditional English or Scottish Hogmanay celebration. The whole school could be asked to think out their personal and corporate New Year resolutions. These could be written on a large piece of card and reviewed at intervals to see whether promises can be kept.

Each celebration could end with a simple prayer of thanks for the old year and a request for God's blessing on the New Year.

Hymn

No. 25, 'A New Year has started', by M. Martin and V. Stumbles (Holt, Rinehart and Winston); or No. 58, 'New things to do' and No. 62, 'Diwali' in *Tinder-box 66 Songs for Children*, (A. and C. Black) or No. 122, 'Shalom Chaverim' in *New Life* (Galliard).

5–7
Assembly

Sunrise

Read Psalm 113:3 (*RSV*), 'From the rising of the sun to its setting the name of the Lord is to be praised.'

The following idea could be the basis of a class tableau that gradually builds up and includes every child.

One child wears a simple 'sandwich board' structure. One side is pitch black; the other side is a golden sun. The tableau begins by the child standing in the centre of the stage, black side towards the rest of the children and gradually, as the words of scripture are read aloud, the child turns around so that the full sun faces the children. A few children, with yellow/gold crepe paper attached to their arms, join the child in the centre and extend their arms at different angles to represent the radiating rays of the sun. Simple masks are needed for the rest of the children as they build up the picture of sunrise.

An owl flits across the stage with a gentle hoot and goes to sleep at one side, signifying the end of night. Cockerels with fine combs and tails strut and crow to mark the beginning of a new day and then they stand still. Other tiny birds with different masks dance in the dawn chorus, before taking their positions around the sun. Rabbits scamper across the stage and begin feeding and washing (simple ears and powder puffs can be worn). Other animals could be added. Man wakes up. The city bursts into life (the song 'Who will buy this beautiful morning?' could be played as children re-enact selling their wares).

The teacher should explain that the rising of the sun heralds God's gift of a new day — a new beginning — a new chance to do something worthwhile.

End with a simple prayer about making the most of the opportunities that are presented to us today. The children could be encouraged to think of helpful or thoughtful acts that they might pursue.

Hymn

No. 6, 'I have seen the golden sunshine' in *Someone's Singing Lord* (A. and C. Black) or No. 13, 'We praise you for the sun', in *Someone's Singing Lord* (A. and C. Black).

2   Places of Worship

5–7
Activity

Exploring a Typical English Church

Love, joy and peace almost seem to go out of the window, as every busy teacher knows, when preparing for Christmas in school. Yet it should not be so. In our rush to prepare cards, decorations, calendars and mammoth Christmas productions, nerves become tattered, children become weary, Christmas seems to lose some of its meaning and what happens to the usual work?

To explore a theme centred on a typical English church may be a slightly less harrowing approach to Christmas in school and yet still include all the necessary skills, attitudes, knowledge and concepts, without much of the agony.

For some children, Christmas will be the only time they will visit a church. How can the experience be made more meaningful; what needs to be done in preparation for the visit; how can it be followed up?

Preparation

1 The teacher needs to visit the local church first on her own, making sure that the layout is known, that something is known about the church architecture, furniture, history, etc., and the provision of toilets.

2 Talk to the minister, perhaps invite him to a school assembly to talk about some interesting features of the church prior to the children's visit. Perhaps he could bring his special robes and talk about them.

3 Show slides of the local church pointing out interesting features.

4 Decide how the project work is to be tackled — by individuals, small groups or the whole class. Very young children may find it simpler to work in small groups with a parent helper, concentrating on one particular aspect of the church. Then the whole class could come together at the end of the project to share their findings. Older infants may like to have a prepared work-sheet of items to look for and then concentrate on and research one particular aspect of the church that interests them — or make their own project book about the artefacts.

5 Allow approximately half an hour for the visit by the younger children. Older children may need a little longer.

TYPICAL ENGLISH CHURCH

Art and Craft

Rubbings — brasses
walls
floors
doors
locks

Printing: white paint on black paper

Model of a church out of a shoe box.
Nativity scene out of plastic salt containers.
Large fabric collage of Holy Family.
Stained glass windows out of tissue paper.
Potato wreaths.
Doily angels, mobiles, stars.
A frieze of mice.

RE

Christmas story.
Christingle service.
Interview a vicar.
Make a collection for a specific charity such
as Save the Children Fund.
Nativity model.
Light — (a topic worth studying in greater
depth another time).

Story/Poetry

J. Goodall, *Naughty Nancy, the Bad
Bridesmaid* (Macmillan 1983) (5-year-olds).
G. Oakley, *The Church Mouse* ((Macmillan,
1972) top infants).
G. Oakley, *The Church Mice at Christmas*
(Macmillan 1980) (top Infants).
C. Mattingley, *The Angel with a Mouth-organ*
(Hodder and Stoughton 1985)
(7–8-year-olds).
J. and G. Adamson, *Topsy and Tim's Sunday
Book* (Blackie 1977) (5-year-olds).

Writing/Reading/Language/Discussion

Make different shaped books, i.e.

The vicar is

The font is

Individual books of what to look for inside/
outside a church (See Figures 2 and 3). Class
books recording the visit. Concertina books
developing a sequence of events — order of
Christmas service, baptism, etc.
*Make a people book. Read parish records,
baptismal roll. What do our names mean?

Maths

Look for different shapes — circles, triangles,
squares, etc. Count doors, windows.
Arbitrary measurement, i.e. handspans,
cubits.
Goliath was six cubits and a span high.
Time: day, night, winter, summer, etc.
Clock face.
Money — how is the church money used?
Symmetry — look for patterns.

Science

Water — what is it used for?
Sound — who or what makes the sound?
Heat — Some objects feel warmer/colder
than others. Make comparisons in church.
Structures — look at shapes, squares,
rectangles, roof, spire, etc.
Property of materials — what is it made of?
Wind — weathercock — which way is the
wind blowing?
Air and burning — candles
Patterns of environment — day and night,
seasons, clocks.
Weather — snow and ice, sun, rain, wind.
Nature study — what does the churchyard
look like at Christmas — plants, trees, birds,
insects?
(See also Figure 3.)

Music

Listen to church music — organ, piano,
instruments, etc. Learn carols. Make own
instruments.

Displays in the classroom

A bell display — encourage the children to
bring in different bells.
Christening gown display.
Photographs of babies — guess who?
Christmas cards display.

People who go to Church

Vicar
Curate
Sidesmen
Masons
Cleaners
Church warden
Bellringers
Sunday School
Congregation
Carpenters
Builders
Gardeners
Flower arrangers
Organist
Church Council
Youth club

Figure 2   What to Look for at a Church

Inside the church		Outside the church	
Font	Roof	Shape of church	Garden
Baptismal roll	Organ	Windows	Trees
Windows	Kneelers	Weather-cock	Headstones
Lectern	Candles	Porch	Roof
Bibles	Tapestries	Doors	Belfry
Pews	Treasures	Walls	Gargoyles
Doors/handles	Pillars	Arches	Gates
Brasses	Decorations	Clock	Notices
Bells	Tombs	Tower or spire	Flowers
Altar	Robes		
Crosses	Inscriptions		
Pulpit	Flowers		
Choir stalls			

Note: A very simple and useful book is R.H.C. Fice and I.M. Simkiss *We discover the Church,* (E.J. Arnold, 1972).

6   Prepare the children by asking them to stand quite still inside the church and listen to the quietness. Remind them not to shout or run about, but to treat the place with respect.

7   Find out about other places of worship in the area. Perhaps a follow-up study could be made next term.

Developing the Theme

Figures 1–3 provides suggestions for developing this theme. Ways of developing some of the aspects referred to in Figures 1–3 are described in more detail below.

Writing

1   Younger children could make simple books with just one sentence on each page. To add interest, they might make different shaped books such as the following.

The vicar is

Figure 3 Use Your Senses to Explore the Church

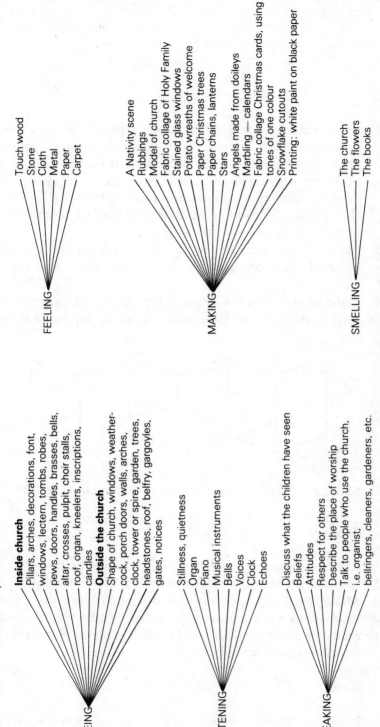

FEELING
- Touch wood
- Stone
- Cloth
- Metal
- Paper
- Carpet

MAKING
- A Nativity scene
- Rubbings
- Model of church
- Fabric collage of Holy Family
- Stained glass windows
- Potato wreaths of welcome
- Paper Christmas trees
- Paper chains, lanterns
- Stars
- Angels made from doileys
- Marbling — calendars
- Fabric collage Christmas cards, using tones of one colour
- Snowflake cutouts
- Printing: white paint on black paper

SMELLING
- The church
- The flowers
- The books

SEEING

Inside church
Pillars, arches, decorations, font, windows, lectern, tombs, robes, pews, doors, handles, brasses, bells, altar, crosses, pulpit, choir stalls, roof, organ, kneelers, inscriptions, candles

Outside the church
Shape of church, windows, weathercock, porch doors, walls, arches, clock, tower or spire, garden, trees, headstones, roof, belfry, gargoyles, gates, notices

LISTENING
- Stillness, quietness
- Organ
- Piano
- Musical instruments
- Bells
- Voices
- Clock
- Echoes

SPEAKING
- Discuss what the children have seen
- Beliefs
- Attitudes
- Respect for others
- Describe the place of worship
- Talk to people who use the church, i.e. organist, bellringers, cleaners, gardeners, etc.

The font is

2　Older children could research one aspect (windows, kneelers) or make their own 'project' book about as many as possible of the items they have seen. The writing need not be long. Time might be better spent drawing from real life observation. Perhaps a mother could take a small group of children back to re-visit the church once the children have decided how to develop their project in order to draw more detailed pictures.

3　Make a class book using items for sale in the church such as postcards, a short history, church magazine to record the class visit.

4　Make a concertina book to develop the idea of a sequence of events such as the order of Christmas service or baptismal service:

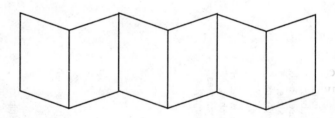

5　Make a 'people' book of all the people who use the church.

Reading

1　Read any notices, inscriptions on the walls or floors.
2　Read parish records, baptismal roll, Roll of Honour.
3　Make word lists that can be suspended from the ceiling in the classroom or put onto language master cards or the computer.
4　Find out about the signs, symbols, tapestries in the church. What do the symbols mean?

Maths

1　Look for different shapes: circles, triangles, squares, etc. Look for symmetry in the building itself.

2 Count doors, windows, pews, etc.
3 Measure in hand spans and cubits. Goliath was 'six cubits and a span' high (approximately 10 feet tall; 1 Samuel 17:4). How far up the wall could he have reached?
4 Time: Can you read the church clock? What do the numerals look like?
5 Money: How is the money spent? Perhaps the children could ask to see the last treasurer's report. This is freely available to anyone who asks and makes interesting reading.

Science

1 Heat: Some objects feel warmer than other objects. Make comparisons in the church. Try touching a wooden pew and a metal rail. Which feels warmer?
2 Structures: look at shapes in the church. Can you see squares, circles, rectangles, etc.? Look at the roof, spire, pillars, columns and arches. Discuss the shape of the structure.
3 Properties of materials: compare surfaces. What is it made of? Discuss strength of different materials.
4 Wind: look for a weathercock. Which way is the wind blowing?
5 Air and burning: light candles and demonstrate how oxygen is used up by covering the candle with an extinguisher.
6 Environmental patterns: day and night, the seasons, months of the year. What does the church look like at these different times?
7 Nature study: What is growing in the churchyard? Are there birds, insects, trees and flowers, etc.?

Art/Craft

1 *A Nativity scene*
   (i) Use plastic salt drums for the bodies. These need to be weighted with small stones or plasticine to prevent them toppling over. To give the effect of two people kneeling, two salt drums could be cut down in size. Once again, plasticine is needed at the base to steady them.
   (ii) Heads can be made out of paper balls covered with old pairs of tights, or plasticine heads can be made.
   (iii) Clothes can be made out of pieces of brightly coloured materials draped around the bodies and glued with a strong glue.

19

(iv)   The scene can then be assembled in the traditional way. (*Note*: a very useful book is M. Hutchings, *Making New Testament Toys* (Mills and Boon, 1972.)

2   *Rubbings*

(i)   You will need paper — experiment with different weights and colours; wax crayons or cobblers wax; adhesive tape to prevent the paper slipping; a small brush to brush away any dirt before you start, that would spoil the effect of the rubbing.

(ii)   Look out for interesting patterns to rub. If the church has brasses, permission needs to be obtained from the vicar. A small fee may be charged.

(iii)   If there are no brasses, try rubbing different textures — walls (look for crusader crosses), floors, doors, masons' marks, locks, etc.

3   *Make a 3-D model of the church*

(i)   Using a ground floor plan (see Appendix) and an old shoe box as the basic church shape, make models of the items inside the church, with a roof that can be lifted off so that everything inside can be seen.

(ii)   Lots of waste materials will be needed to make the pews, altar, font, etc.

4   *Fabric collage of the Holy Family*

(i)   Simple outline shapes may be needed to guide the youngest children. Use the picture of the east window at Hailsham parish church to help you work out the nativity scene (see page 26). Perhaps the older children could look at this picture and make their own collage without the teacher's help.

(ii)   Lots of different coloured fabric will be needed to make the 'stained glass window' effect. Also use some strong glue.

5   *Small stained glass window Christmas cards*

(i)   Tissue paper, glue and strong card will be needed.

(ii)   The youngest children can just stick the tissue paper onto card in an abstract design. Older children may like to make a real stained glass window by cutting out the basic shape and decorating with tissue paper. (See *Bright Ideas for Christmas Art and Craft* (Ward Lock Educational/Scholastic, 1984)).

6   *Potato wreaths and table decorations*

(i)   These are so simple to make, yet very effective. All that is needed are some large potatoes, holly, tinsel and a ribbon.

(ii) Press the holly into the potato and intertwine the tinsel, tie on the red ribbon.

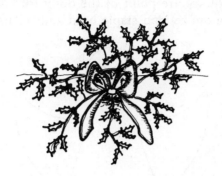

(iii) Smaller potatoes can be used with smaller pieces of foliage and a candle to make a table decoration.

7 *Mobiles of stars and angels*
   (i) To make the angels you will need one pretty white paper doily per child, a stapler and a piece of paper for the head and wings.
   (ii) The child makes a round face

   Wings can be drawn

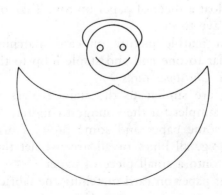

and covered with 'mosaic' pieces of brightly coloured sticky paper.

(iii) Take the centre point of the doily (or cut it in half if trying to economize) and staple head and wings to the body.

(iv) Stars can be cut out (see *Bright Ideas for Christmas Art and Craft* (Ward Lock Educational/Scholastic, 1984)) and covered with 'mosaic' pieces of silver foil.

(v) Assemble together to make a mobile.

8   *Marbling calendars*

(i) Use little tins of enamel paint (the type used to paint model aircraft). You will need a deep tray of water and a straw to take up little blobs of different coloured paint. Choose two colours at a time. Swirl the paint around on top of the water, then float a sheet of paper on top. Take off the paper quickly and leave to dry.

(ii) Mount marble picture on card matching for tone. Staple calendar to one end and staple loop to the other end.

9   *Fabric collage Christmas cards*

(i) These are similar to the stained glass window cards, but much simpler for the youngest children. You will need some card, some paper and some pretty fabric. Using only one tone (e.g. all blues or all greens), let the children stick the fabric onto a small piece of paper.

(ii) Mount paper on card matching the fabric, e.g. *blue* fabric or white paper mounted on *blue* card.

Figure 4 summarizes the skills, attitudes and concepts that can be developed by using this topic.

Figure 4   Skills, Attitudes, Concepts Developed by Activities Relating to a Church

SKILLS	ATTITUDES
Observation	Willingness to ask questions
Describing	Respect for the beliefs of others
Thinking	Respect for the craftsmen and workers of all kinds,
Reflecting	who are motivated by their love of God
Assessing information	Sense of care and responsibility
Presenting	Enjoyment in using all the senses for exploring
Working cooperatively	and discriminating
Speaking	
Listening	
Reading	CONCEPTS
Writing	Size
Understanding	Shape
Imagining	Church artefacts
Understanding use of symbolism	The church in the community
Computing	Sense of awe and wonder
Experimenting	Awareness of meaning of words

Resources

Reference Books

BENNETT, O. *Exploring Religion: Buildings* (Bell and Hyman 1984).
BROWN, J. *History Explorers: Churches* (A. and C. Black 1983).
COLE, O. *Come inside the Church* (six religions). (Studio Vista 1974).
FICE, R.H.C. and SIMKISS I.M. *We Discover the Church* (E.J. Arnold 1972).
FLETCHER, H.J. *The First Book of Bells* (E. Ward 1965).
HUNT, P.J. *What to Look for inside a Church* (Ladybird 1972).
VALE, E *Churches* (Batsford 1957).
YOUNG, M. *Singing Windows* (World's Work 1963).

Art and Craft Books

GRATER, M. *One Piece of Paper* (Mills and Boon 1963) (useful for the mouse frieze as well as nativity figures).
HUTCHINGS, M. *Making New Testament Toys* (Mills and Boon 1972).
HUTCHINGS, M. *Making Old Testament Toys* (Mills and Boon 1972).
SCHOLASTIC MAGAZINES *Bright Ideas for Christmas Art and Craft* (Ward Lock Educational/Scholastic 1984).
SKINNER, M.K. *How to Make Decorations* (Studio Vista 1974).

Assembly Books

DAVIDSON, S. *Infant Assemblies* (Scripture Union 1983).
FISHER, R. *Together with Infants* (Evans Bros 1982).
PRESCOTT, D.M. *More Stories for Infants at Home and School* (Blandford Press 1975).
PURTON, R. and STOREY, C. *First Assemblies* (Blackwell 1981).

Story Books

ADAMSON, J. & G. *Topsy and Tim's Sunday Book* (Blackie 1977) (reception infants).
GOODALL, J.S. *Naughty Nancy, the Bad Bridesmaid* (Macmillan 1983).
MATTINGLEY, C. *The Angel with a Mouth-organ* (Hodder and Stoughton 1985). (suitable for 7–8-year-olds, a very sad story with a happy ending, well worth reading to older children).
OAKLEY, G. *The Church Mice at Christmas* (Macmillan 1980) (top infants).
OAKLEY, G. *The Church Mouse* (Macmillan 1972) (excellent vocabulary and language structure, lovely humour, suitable for top infants).
SEUSS, DR. *How the Grinch Stole Christmas* (Collins 1973) (suitable for middle-top infant children; if you are a fan of Dr Seuss, you will enjoy reading this book to your class).

Poetry Books

McWILLIAMS, J. *Sing, Say and Move* (Scripture Union 1981) a book of action songs, games and rhymes for the under 8's.
WOODLAND E.J.M. *Poems for Movement* (Evans Bros 1966).

Audiovisual Aids

FILMSTRIPS *The Christmas Story* (Philip Green Educational) Ref. No. F26.
POSTERS *Christian Festivals* (S4) Ref. E745 and *Birth Rites* (S4) Ref. E720 (both published by Pictorial Charts Educational Trust); Benedictine Nuns of Cockfosters, *The Life of Christ* (Nelsons' Bible Visual Aids).
SLIDES *Jesus the Child* (Ladybird/Scripture Union).

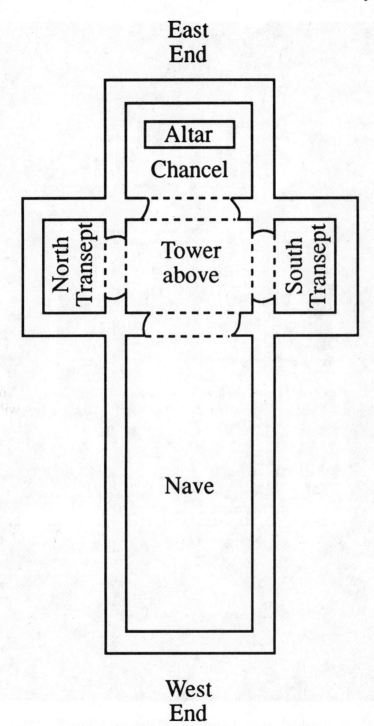

Appendix: Ground Plan of a Church

Stained glass window, Maisham Church

The Christingle Service

It is usually a good idea to alternate a mammoth production with a 'quiet' event. In this way teachers and children do not try to out-do each other each year and the Christmas event becomes really enjoyable. Parents enjoy it too, especially when they can join in by singing the well known carols. Mothers and fathers might also be asked to read the lessons.

A lovely service, which does not require masses of costumes, but simply an orange, a candle, some fruits or sweets and a red ribbon for each child, is the Christingle service. The Christingle originated in Czechoslovakia and is now held for children all over the world.

Briefly, each child needs a decorated orange as a reminder of what Christmas is all about. The round orange represents the world. A candle is placed into the top of the orange to represent Jesus, the Light of the World. Four cocktail sticks with sweets or raisins are pushed into the orange to represent the four corners of the earth — north, south, east and west — where the Light of the World reaches. The sweets or raisins represent all the good things of the earth that come to us from God. Finally, the red ribbon is tied around the orange to remind us that Jesus came to die for us.

In a proper Christingle service all the lights in the church would be turned off and each child holding a Christingle would have their candles lit. However, in cramped and difficult conditions with few adults to supervise it may be sensible just to let the older children stand at the end of each pew and have their candles lit. The service is very simple: carols interspersed with readings, an explanation about the orange, a final carol and then the candles are all blown out.

5–7
Assembly

A Closer Look Inside and Outside A Church

Following the ideas outlined on pages 14–26 the children can present an assembly using the detailed studies of their findings. Each child should be given a different aspect of the church to study, draw or paint (see Figure 5). Perhaps models could be made. At the assembly each child can be given an opportunity to hold up his/her painting and read a short descriptive piece about what he or she has discovered.

Prayers

Father, We thank you that through the ages men have toiled with their hands, minds and bodies, to create something of beauty to bring glory to you and lasting pleasure to others. Amen.

Hymn

No. 19, He gave me eyes so I could see', in *Someone's Singing Lord* (A. and C. Black).

Figure 5 Aspects of the church for further study

Inside	Outside
Altar	Churchyard
Pulpit	Trees/shrubs
Font	Flowers
Pews	Spire
Lectern	Gargoyles
Stained glass windows	Weathervanes
Brasses	Porch
Tombs	
Bells	
Organ	
Symbols (see pp. 30–34)	
Banners	

People Who Use the Church

This activity is designed for a class assembly involving every child. The props are simple: headdresses, and labels could be worn to indicate each character:

Vicar
Sidesmen
Choir
Bellringers
Flower ladies/men
Gardeners
Cleaning ladies/men
PCC
Parents and baby for baptism
Couple for wedding
Mourners for funeral (this could be left out if very young children are present)
Congregation

The scene could be built up gradually as each child enters with a brief description of what he/she does:

First child as vicar: I am the vicar; it is my job to care for all the people in this neighbourhood and to oversee every aspect of church life. These are the people who help me.

Sidesmen: We are the sidesmen; we welcome the people and show them to their seats. We also help to look after the building and see that everything runs smoothly.

Choir: We are the choir. We praise God through our singing. We not only sing at all the services, but we have to do a lot of practices during the week.

In small churches a choir may be made up of just a few people, but in a cathedral the complete choir may be sixty people or more.

Bellringers: We are the bellringers. We also have to practise during the week. Before services on Sunday, we ring the bells to tell the people that the service is about to begin. We also ring our bells after weddings in celebration, and on other special occasions like the birth of a royal baby.

Flower ladies: It is our job to decorate the church and make it look beautiful. We make sure that there are fresh flowers in all the vases. At special times of the year like Christmas, Easter and Harvest we do special floral displays:

Gardeners: We are the gardeners. We have to mow the lawns and keep the flower beds free from weeds.

Cleaners: We clean the church [each child could describe a different aspect of the work]: I polish the brasses; I clean the windows; I scrub the floors; I dust the pews; I sweep the paths.

PCC: I am a member of the Parochial Church Council. I help the vicar with difficult decisions and I look after the church funds. I am called the PCC Treasurer.

Parents, baby and godparents: We are bringing our baby to be baptised. We are going to call her Georgina [or insert the name of a new baby brother or sister of one of the children in school].

Couple for wedding: The minister is going to perform our wedding ceremony. We know him well because he has talked to us about what marriage means and the promises we shall make to each other and to God.

Mourners: We feel very sad because our old friend has died. But the vicar has arranged a joyful 'Thanksgiving Service' for our friend. We shall remember all the good things he did and give thanks to God for his life.

[Last child points to the school]

Congregation: Finally, all of us make up the congregation. Without us the church would be empty. Lots of different people come to the church: young and old, short and tall, different coloured people. God loves each one of us.

Prayer

Heavenly Father, Help each one of us to discover our own talents, whether it is gardening or singing, or caring for others, and enable us to offer this talent back to you in thanksgiving. Amen.

Hymn

No. 37, 'Working together', in *Every Colour under the Sun* (Ward Lock Educational).

Music

'I'd like to teach the world to sing'.

5–9
Assembly

Interview A Local Minister

Invite the local minister to the school. If the school serves a multi-faith area, invite one or two other ministers into the school in turn. Explain to the children that in all places of worship there is a leader.

Let the children prepare interview questions to ask the visitor on the day. Try to draw out different aspects of his job.

1   How many services are there on the day of worship?
2   Whom does he visit — the sick, elderly, infirm?
3   What happens during the week — how many meetings, services, funerals, weddings, baptisms does he attend?
4   When does the minister have a day off?
5   What does he like to do on his day off?
6   What does the church offer to children, young people, families, the elderly?
7   How long does it take to prepare a sermon?
8   Does the church have links overseas?
9   Why does the church have jumble sales, etc.?
10   Which hymns are his favourites?

Having elicited this information, perhaps the school could sing the minister's favourite hymn.

If this idea is extended to include ministers from other faiths, charts could be drawn up listing the different or similar activities that each minister engages in.

Prayer

No. 11, p. 195 in *First Assemblies* (Blackwell).

Hymn

Chosen by minister or No. 23 in *Someone's Singing Lord* 'Kum Ba Yah' (A. and C. Black).

Colours: Saints, Signs and Symbols

(Illustrations and quotations from W. Ellwood Post *Saints, Signs and Symbols* (Morehouse Barlow Co., 1962 and 1974) (reproduced by permission of SPCK).

Begin with five dancers, each with coloured cloth attached at the backs, spreading out to the little fingers of each hand. The colours needed are black, blue, green, purple and white. The children can improvise their own movement before coming to rest and explaining the significance of their own colour.

The following explanations are generally accepted interpretations of the significance of colours as used by the church: —
Black — solemnity, death
Blue — traditional colour of Mary, the Virgin
Green — Spring, triumph of life over death
Purple— Royalty, imperial power (God the Father)
White — Purity, holiness

Five more children could wear the colours worn by religious orders and find out something about each one to tell the rest of the children.

Black — The Benedictines, Augustinians, Jesuits, Cowley Fathers.
Gray — The Franciscans.
White — The reformed branch of the Benedictines, Cistercians, the Order of the Holy Cross.
Black over White — The Dominicans.
White over Brown — The Carmelites.

Four children could paint the following symbols and explain their significance:

Holy Trinity — a circle within a triangle

God the Father — hand of God

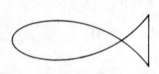

God the Son — a Christian symbol used from the first century as a secret sign; the Greek initials of 'Jesus Christ, Son of God, Saviour' make up the Greek word for fish

God the Holy Spirit

Three or more children could hold up copies of sacred monograms:

IHS

The first three letters of the Greek word for Jesus

The first two letters of the Greek word 'Christos', meaning Christ.

INRI

The initial letters of the Latin words 'Jesus Nazarenus Rex Judaeorum', Jesus of Nazareth, the King of the Jews (John 19: 19–22).

Four or more children could make studies of the emblems most commonly associated with certain saints. The following are just a few; there are many more suggestions in Post's *Saints, Signs and Symbols.*

St Augustine of Canterbury (7th century) 'Member of the Benedictine Order and the first Archbishop of Canterbury. Silver Cross, gold pall, silver lily on a black field' (Post, *op. cit.*). He is remembered on 26 May. The Story about how he came to England from Rome can be found in C. Alexander, *The Church's Year* (Oxford University Press). London 1950.

St Boniface (8th Century) 'The Archbishop of Mentz established the foundation for Christianity in Germany. His emblem refers to his defence of the Gospel as he met the blow of death while confirming baptized converts. A gold book, sword with gold hilt and silver blade, on a red field' (Post, *op. cit.*) He is remembered on 5 June (see Alexander, *op. cit.*).

35

St Cecilia (3rd century) 'The only apparent reason for her to be known as the patroness of Music, is that St. Cecilia is said to have been skilled in singing the divine praises, oft accompanied by an instrument. A gold harp, with silver strings, on a blue field' (Post, *op. cit.*). She is remembered on 22 November.

St John Baptist (1st century) 'The last of the Jewish prophets, who prepared the way for the coming of Jesus Christ. The Maltese Cross of silver, on a black field, is also the emblem of the Venerable Order of the Hospital of St John of Jerusalem' (*ibid*). He is remembered on 24 June. The exciting story of his birth, the baptism of Jesus and his death can be read in the Bible and is simply re-told in Alexander, *op. cit.*

Five or more children could hold up different shaped crosses and explain where they originate.

Canterbury

Latin

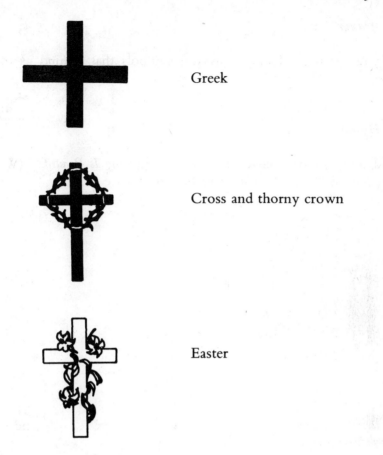

Greek

Cross and thorny crown

Easter

Finally, a study could be made of some of the flowers, fruits and tree symbols that are used in churches. Their meaning and significance could be rediscovered and related to the rest of the children.

'The Apple means salvation when shown in the hand of Jesus Christ; and sin, when shown in the hand of Adam.' (Post, *op. cit.*).

'The Bulrush means hope of salvation to the faithful' (Post, *op. cit.*). (Job 8: 11–13)

Prayer

Thank you for the colours, signs and symbols that remind us of your presence.

Hymn

'The old rugged cross' on record Dana, *Everything Is Beautiful*' (Warwick records, No. W.W. 5099, also available on cassette.

7–11
Assembly

Christianity Around the World

Read Romans 12: 4–5 (*RSV*) 'For as in one body we have many members, and all the members do not have the same function, so we, though many, are one body in Christ, and individually members one of another.'

Before this assembly the teacher will need to study Part 14 Background Information for teachers, on different Christian denominational faiths and practices. Christians around the world share the same basic belief, that there is one God and Jesus Christ is His Son. Therefore, Christians everywhere, despite their differences in style of worship, are all members of the world-wide body of Jesus Christ.

This assembly could either focus on each faith in turn and therefore be spread over many weeks, or be the culmination of many weeks' work, to show what has been learnt about each style of worship. Either way, much careful preparation is needed, and each faith should not only be looked at from the point of view of worship in Great Britain, but how the faith is practised, say, in the West Indies — what it means to be a Pentecostal in Jamaica, or a Roman Catholic in Italy, or an Orthodox Christian in Greece.

If possible, an attempt should be made to display pictures, maps, artefacts, traditional costumes, etc. from the country 'visited' each week. Draw on children's own holiday experiences abroad or use pictures from travel agents. Set up a display table depicting each country that can be changed each week. Finally, let each member of the class dress up in the traditional costume of different countries or wear a simple label and say a brief word about the Christian 'Church' he is representing.

Prayer

Father God, We thank you that we are all part of your world-wide family, united through our Lord, Jesus Christ. Amen.

Hymn

No. 19, 'He's got the whole world in his Hands', in *Every Colour under the Sun* (Ward Lock Educational).

Resources

Reference Books

BATES, J. *Visiting a Methodist Church* (Lutterworth Educational, 1984).

BATES, S. *Religions of the World* (Macdonald Educational, 1985).

BENNETT, O. *Festivals* (Bell and Hyman, 1986).

BENNETT, O. *People* (Bell and Hyman, 1985).

BENNETT, O. *Worship* (Bell and Hyman, 1984). (There are many more books in this series.)

BLACKWELL, M. *Visiting a Salvation Army Citadel* (Lutterworth Educational, 1984).

BROWN, A. *The Christian World* (Macdonald, 1984).

CALDWELL, J.C. *Let's Visit the West Indies* (Burke, 1972).

CAMPBELL, K. *The Caribbean* (Macdonald Educational, 1983).

COCAGNAC, A.M. *When I Go to Mass* (Macmillan, 1965).

COLLINSON, C. and MILLER, C. *Celebrations* (Edward Arnold, 1985).

HARRISON, S.W. and SHEPHERD, D. *A Christian Family in Britain* (RMEP, 1986).

HOBLEY, L.F. *Christians and Christianity* (Wayland, 1979).

KILLINGRAY, M. *I Am an Anglican* (Franklin Watts, 1986).

KNUTSSON, B. *Christianity* (Hulton Press, 1985).

LAWTON, C.A. *Shap Calendar of Religious Festivals* (Commission for Racial Equality, 1987).

LONG, R. *The Lutheran Church* (RMEP, 1984). (There are many more books in the Christian Denomination Series).

LYE, K. *Let's Go to Jamaica* (Franklin Watts, 1988). (There are many more books in this series.)

MARTIN, N. *Christianity* (Wayland, 1985).

MAYLED, J. *Pilgrimage* (Wayland, 1986).

MAYLED, J. *Religious Dress* (Wayland, 1987). (There are more books in this series.)

PETTENUZZO, B. *I Am a Roman Catholic* (Franklin Watts, 1985).

PETTENUZZO, B. *I Am a Pentecostal* (Franklin Watts, 1986).

PURTON, R.W. *Churches and Religions* (Blandford Press, 1972).

ROUSSOU, M. *I Am a Greek Orthodox* (Franklin Watts, 1985).

RYE, J. *The Story of the Christians* (Cambridge University Press, 1986).

SHAP WORKING PARTY *World Religions in Education, Festivals* (Commission for Racial Equality, 1987).

THOMAS, R. and STUTCHBURY, J. *The Pope and the Vatican* (Macdonald, 1986).

THORLEY, S. *Christianity in Words and Pictures* (RMEP, 1984).

WARD, M. *Protestant Christian Churches* (Ward Lock Educational, 1970).

WRIGHT, C. *The Christian Churches* (Batsford Academic and Educational, 1982).

Audio-visual Aids

Posters Christian Festivals (Pictorial Charts Educational Trust, No. E745) (covers Christmas, Easter, Whitsun and Harvest).

Nelson's Bible Visual Aids (T. Nelson and Sons), (sets A, B and C cover the birth, life and death of Jesus).

Soundstrips Luke Street (Scripture Union), (eight occasions when Jesus meets different people, taken from Luke's Gospel, beautifully re-told by Roy Castle and intended for 7–11-year-olds).

The Champion (Scripture Union) (portrays the Easter story in modern form (for 11–13-year-olds), with lovely music by Garth Hewitt; parts could be shown to younger children, e.g. when Jesus washes his disciples' feet).

3   Friends and Neighbours

7–9
Activity

Friends and Neighbours: Discussion and Activities

It is important to encourage children to look at those closest to them, to value the family, friends and those at school who love and care for children. Children need to *work* at building up good relationships with those with whom they come into daily contact. They need to learn that true friendship comes through give and take, through not always insisting on their own way, through putting others before themselves.

In these assemblies children are asked to think about their friends; what makes a friend and how they can be a *true* friend. It is hoped that children will come to realize that people are worth more than treasured *things*. *People* are the real treasures in a world that places great emphasis on material things.

Discussion Points

1 Stress how important a friendship is, perhaps a lifelong treasure.
2 Importance of brothers and sisters, remaining friends because they share so much common experience.
3 Importance of mothers, fathers, aunts, uncles, grandmothers, grandfathers and someone special who understands you and whom you understand; a treasured relationship.
4 What is a friend? What makes you like one another? Whom can you trust?
5 A friend in God.
6 Hidden treasure in ourselves — our talents, discuss the variety of contributions that each of us can make. What 'piece of treasure' could we offer to our school, our home, our community?

Follow-up Activities for Children

Written Work

1 Write about your special person. What qualities do they have? What do they look like? Why are they so special?
2 Write about yourself honestly. What are your good points? What

are your bad points? Make happy/sad masks and write a piece of prose, noting your ten good points and your ten worst faults (see also 'The Good Me and the Bad Me' idea on p. 61). Use these as the basis for a school assembly.

3 Write a puppet play for kind characters and wicked characters. Think about what makes someone good and what makes someone bad. Think of a story line with 'good' triumphing at the end.

Religious and Moral Education

1 Stress the many qualities that make someone a 'treasure' or qualities that we should value — those who are caring, those who comfort, those who listen, those who give generously of their time, talents and money.

2 Jesus told a story about using your talents (Luke 19: 11–26); see modern version, 'P. Burbridge and M. Watts in 'Time to Act' (Hodder and Stoughton Limited, 1979).

3 Look at Paul's teaching on what makes a person special. Read Romans 12: 9–21 on how to treat someone who has wronged you; or I Corinthians 13: 1–13 about real love.

4 Point out that people with these special qualities are worth more than gold; moreover, their deeds will be remembered long after they are dead. See some of the 'great lives' discussed in Part 12.

5 Discuss the use of your tongue — how something unkind can never be unsaid; how a lie can only make matters worse; but how a kind word might be remembered for the rest of a person's life.

6 Look at some of the wise sayings in the Old Testament such as Proverbs or the wise sayings of Solomon; make a book of 'wise sayings'.

Music

Listen to the tape of *Godspell*, music and lyrics by Stephen Schwartz, especially the part about storing up treasure on earth.

Art/Craft

1 Make happy and sad masks out of cardboard boxes or paper bags.
2 Make papier-mâché puppets of good and evil characters.
3 Paint a picture of your friend (see page 47).

Resources

BEANEY, J. *Fun with Collage* (Kaye and Ward, 1972).

BRANDLING, R. *Assembly Poems and Prose* (Macmillan, 1977) (includes several poems about treasure).

BRECKON, A. and PREST, D. *Craft, Design and Technology* (Hutchinson, 1983) (for funny faces).

GRATER, M. *Complete Book of Paper Mask Making* , Dover Books, 1984.

MCKELLAR, S. *My Family* (Evans Bros., 1982) (poems and pictures).

5–11
Assembly

Choosing Friends: Rogues' Gallery

Ask all the children in the class to study their best friend very carefully and to paint a picture of him or her. Explain that the paintings will be used as a 'Rogues' Gallery', so that each one can be identified. The teacher may need to help the child who is friendless, and encourage other children to paint him or her.

Then ask the children why they chose a particular person. What qualities does a friend have? Give some examples of the kind of things they do together. How does one keep friends? What should you do after a quarrel? Write a brief account. The children could hold up their pictures and read a short extract from the descriptions of their friends.

Now tell and mime this story (based on an idea by R. Wood in *Activity Talks with Boys and Girls*, N.C.E.C. 1972) You will need:

A rich man sitting at a table
Some shoppers
Pile of coins
A beautiful robe
A thief
A mother
Her son

(Read Matthew 6: 19–21). There was once a man who became very rich by selling things to other people. [Rich man sells articles to shoppers.] He became so rich that soon he had piles of money. [Rich man counts money.]

He was able to buy himself a beautiful robe. He stored up all his money and he treasured his lovely robe [rich man holds up the robe, puts it on, twirls round in it].

But one night, when he was fast asleep, a thief came and stole his lovely robe and all his money. [Thief creeps in and steals the robe and money.]

When the rich man woke up he had nothing left. He had spent all his life getting rich for nothing. [The rich man wakes up, sees that his robe and money have gone. He buries his head in his hands.]

Now in that same town there was a wise mother and she told her son that she did not mind what he did as long as he made the world a better place to live in. [Mother mimes talking to her son.]

'How can I do that, Mum?' he asked. His mother told him that he must be truthful, kind, gentle and make friends, because no one could steal away kindness, gentleness, truthfulness or friendliness.

Prayer

'Heavenly Father, Help me to see not so much of what I can get out of my friends, but more of what I can give to them. Help me to be kind and gentle and truthful because no one can steal these things away. Amen.

Hymn

No. 31, 'Thank you for my friends', in *Tinder-box: 66 Songs for Children* (A. and C. Black).

Losing Friends

To demonstrate how our hands can be welcoming or rejecting. You will need:

4 children to demonstrate hand positions
Folded newspaper (two pieces)
Pair of scissors

The teacher could begin in the following way. Using the scissors she cuts out the shape of some paper dolls and explains that she wants to make a paper chain of friends joining hands together.

For the first demonstration, she deliberately cuts through where the hands should join. The paper children fall to the floor.

She asks the children what has gone wrong.

She takes a second piece of newspaper and this time she is very careful to ensure that the hands will remain joined.

Two children can hold up the chain of dolls between them.

The teacher should go on to explain that friendship is a bit like the joined hands. When hands are joined together, it generally means love, friendship, fun and games. When hands are not joined together, it generally means broken friendship. The friends become a bit like the paper dolls on the floor — alone, sad and lost.

Now ask the four children to come forward and using their hands, mime the following actions:

punching
hitting
pinching
smacking

The teacher should explain that these actions are all hurtful, unkind, and the quickest way to lose friends.

Now the four children can demonstrate ways of using their hands in a kindly way:

Caring hands   — putting their hands round their friend's shoulder;

Helping hands   — lifting a heavy bag;

Fun hands   — playing cat's cradle or turning a skipping rope;

Beckoning hands — welcoming new children to join a game of 'Ring a Ring o' Roses'.

Now read the poem written by a 10-year-old girl entitled 'Loneliness from R. Deadman and A. Razzell, Awareness 2: (Macmillan Education 1977).

Loneliness

I sit on the side of the pavement,
watching.
How I wish I hadn't broken friends
She's got everybody on her side
I wish, I wish she'd let me play
The lump in my throat aches
It feels as though its going to burst
Any moment now.
My eyes are swimming with tears —
I opened my mouth to shout,
'Susan, can I play?'
No sound came out.
I couldn't stand it any longer,
I buried my face in my hands
And quietly wept.

(Tracey Stevens, aged 10)

Prayer

'Heavenly Father, Grant today that we do not quarrel with our friends c make anyone as unhappy as the little girl in the poem. Help us to stretc out our hands and join them in friendship. Make our hands kind an helpful and caring. Amen.

Hymn

No. 30, 'You'll sing a song and I'll sing a song', in *Tinder-box: 66 Songs f Children* (A. and C. Black) (this hymn encourages the children to add furth verses of their own) or No. 36, 'Look out for loneliness', in *Someon Singing Lord* (A. and C. Black).

Losing Friends: Discussion and Activities

Written Work

1 Write about what it feels like to be left out, lonely or different. Can you write your own poem?
2 List the ways in which you could turn that situation around and make a person feel wanted, happy, part of the group.
3 Imagine you are wearing someone else's shoes. What sort of shoes would they be?
4 Write about what you are afraid of.

Religious and Moral Education

1 Jesus met a man who was hated and despised, but he made that man feel wanted and loved. The man's name was Zacchaeus and the story can be found in Luke 19: 1–8. Why not show the filmstrip/tape presentation called 'The Cheat's House' in *Luke Street* (Scripture Union) (mentioned on p. 57) Perhaps the children could act out the playlet for an assembly.
2 Look out for a lonely child in your school, your street, your club.
3 Read about the young boy and the lonely old lady in R. Brandling, *Assembly Poems and Prose* (Macmillan 1977); the piece is called 'The Chess Match' (or see 'The Chess Game' adapted by the author on p. 93).
4 Tell the Old Testament story of Joseph, feeling lost, betrayed and alone when he was sold into slavery by his brothers (Genesis 37–45; read selections).

Music

Hymns: No. 36, 'Look out for loneliness, in *Someone's Singing Lord* (A. and C. Black) or No. 32, 'Who's that sitting in a sycamore tree?', in *Someone's Singing Lord* (A. and C. Black).
Song by Andrew Lloyd Webber, 'The Amazing Technicolour Dreamcoat'.

Art/Craft

1 Paint a picture of a lonely person.
2 Make a picture book depicting scenes from Joseph's story. Write a one-line caption underneath.

Resources

ALTHEA, *My New Family* (Dinosaur, 1984) (for 7-year-olds).
HOGAN, P., *Mum, Will Dad Ever Come Back?* (Raintree Publishers, 1980) (for 7-year-olds).
RICE, T. and LLOYD WEBBER, A. *Joseph and the Amazing Technicolour Dreamcoat* (Pavilion Books and Picture Puffin, Reprint 1988).

5–11
Assembly

The Unforgiving Servant

(From P. Burbridge and M. Watts *Time to Act* (Hodder and Stoughton, 1979)

Act out the following play to demonstrate the need to forgive one another in all sorts of relationships. You will need the following characters: Two narrators, King, Servant, Wife, Children, Friend and Two Armed Guards.

One: The disciple Peter said to Jesus:
Two: How often must I forgive someone who hurts me?
One: And Jesus said to Peter:
Two: Think of a number too big to think of.
One: And while Peter was thinking,
Two: Jesus told the following story:
One: The Kingdom of Heaven
Two: Is rather like
One: This.
Two: There was a king.
          (Enter KING computing accounts with a notebook and pencil.)
          Settling accounts with his servants.
One: And there was a servant
Two: Settling accounts with the king.
          (Enter SERVANT with enormous debt hung round his neck.)
One: And the servant owed the king some money.
Two: Quite a lot of money, really.
One: Loads and loads of it, in fact.
Two: Hundreds!
One: Thousands!
Two: Millions!
One: Well anyway, it was a lot of money.
Two: For a chap like him.
One: A massive great big debt.
Two: Hanging round his neck.
One: And he knew that he couldn't pay

Two: And the king knew that he couldn't pay

One: And he knew that the king knew that he knew he couldn't pay.

Two: Which was pretty bad news.

One: So the king ordered him to be sold as a slave.

Two: And his wife

One: And his children

Two: And all that he possessed.

One: To go to the liquidators.

Two: 'Five quid for his shirt!'

One: 'Six quid for his shoes!'

Two: 'Twenty five "p" for his socks!'

One: (Holding his nose). No, leave the socks, mate.

Two: - 'Stop!' he shouted.

One: And he fell on his knees — clunk!

Two: And he implored the king to have patience with him.

One: 'Have patience with me!'

Two: He implored.

One: 'And I will pay you everything!'

Two: A likely story.

One: But seeing the poor man's distress

Two: The king was deeply moved.
      (The KING removes a handkerchief, wipes tears from his eyes, wrings out the handkerchief and replaces it.)

One: In one short moment he forgave the man the whole debt!

Two: The whole lot.
      (The KING strikes out the debt and leaves.)

One: Forgiven,

Two: In a moment.

One: Just like that.

Two: Wow!

One: Cor!

Two: Incredible!

One: Too much!

Two: Needless to say, the man was very pleased

One: And he went on his way, merrily
      (NARRATOR ONE whistles nonchantly).

Two: On his way, he bumped into a friend.
      (Enter FRIEND)

One: Who owed him a fiver.

Two: 'Aha! You owe me five quid,' he cried.

One: Seizing him briskly by the throat.

Two: What do you say to that?

One: (Strangled noise).
Two: That's no excuse!
One: But the man fell on his knees — clunk!
Two: And implored the servant to have patience with him.
One: 'Have patience with me!'
Two: He implored.
One: 'And I will pay you everything!'
Two: But, ignoring the poor man's distress,
One: He flung him into jail
Two: Until the debt was paid in full.
       (The SERVANT drags his friend by the scruff of the neck and throws him off stage.)
One: But the king
Two: Who kept his ears to the ground
       (Enter KING, listening to the ground.)
One: Heard about this
Two: And what he heard made him extremely angry.
One: In anger he summoned the servant before him.
Two: 'You wicked servant!'
One: He said, angrily.
Two: 'Think of all that I forgave you.
One: Think of what you refused to forgive.
Two: I showed you mercy.
One: You showed him none.
Two: Therefore I will show you none'.
One: And the servant was sent to jail.
       (Enter TWO ARMED GUARDS who remove the trembling SERVANT.)
Two: Where he would be very well looked after.
One: (He laughs knowingly). Nya, nya, nya, nya . . .
Two: Until his debt was paid in full.
One: And the king said:
       (The KING comes forward, as if to address the audience.)
Two: 'Think carefully.
One: This will happen to you as well,
Two: If you do not forgive your brother
One: From your heart.'

(N.B. Permission for a *public* performance of this sketch should be obtained from P. Burbridge and M. Watts, P.O. Box 223, York, Y01 1GW.)

Prayer

Father, you always forgive us when we do wrong, and you go on loving us in spite of our misdeeds. Help us to be forgiving to others when they wrong us. Amen.

Hymn

No. 35 'I'm Forgiven', in *Songs of Fellowship* (Kingsway).

The Lion and The Mouse

This mime demonstrates that everyone can help each other. You will need:

Characters	Props
A lion	A lion mask, or neck ruff made out of crêpe paper, a long tail
A mouse	A mouse mask, or a simple pair of ears; whiskers can be painted on face (ideas for masks can be found in M. Grater, *Paper Faces* (Mills and Boon 1967)).
Four hunters	Anoraks or camouflage jackets can be worn
Three (or more) trees	Twig headdress, or crepe paper attached to arms; brown paper wrapped round trunks
One narrator	
	Large piece of netting (fisherman's or garden netting will do)

The main elements of the story are as follows. The narrator sets the scene by telling the children that the stage is the jungle; he points to the trees as they take up their positions [enter trees]. The narrator introduces the lion, who lies down, stretches out and goes to sleep in the sun [enter lion]. The narrator introduces the little mouse who scurries across the stage several times before finally stepping on the lion's tail [enter mouse].

The lion jumps up and shouts, 'How dare you wake me up — I will kill you for this!' Raises paw about to kill the mouse. The mouse cowers. The little mouse pleads with the lion. 'Oh please don't kill me! Some day I might be able to help you.' The lion roars with laughter, 'Oh don't be so silly; how can a little thing like you help me? But, as you are such a funny little mouse, I will let you go this time — only don't wake me up again!'

Narrator: The lion lets the little mouse go [mouse scampers off stage] and the lion goes back to sleep. Just then, four hunters came into the jungle. They were hoping to catch a lion to send to the zoo. They were hoping to get a great deal of money. The hunters set a trap using a huge net. [The hunters hang the net from branches of the trees, then go off stage.]

Narrator: The lion wakes up. Stretches, yawns and goes for a walk. By accident, the lion walks straight into the trap. [The trees throw the net

57

over the lion, who collapses onto the ground.] The lion struggles and struggles to try and get out and at last he gives up, feeling exhausted. The whole jungle could hear his pitiful cries. Suddenly, the little mouse scampers up to the lion and says, 'Let me help you. I can set you free' [enter mouse].

The lion says, 'How can you possibly set me free? If a strong lion like me can't get out of this net, you couldn't possibly help me.' 'Oh yes, I can', says the little mouse.

Narrator: The little mouse began to gnaw through the net, first in one place, then another, then another. Suddenly, the lion is free. The lion thanks the mouse. They shake hands and both scamper off.

The teacher needs to draw the threads together by saying something like: 'Who would have believed that a little tiny mouse could have helped a great big lion? However small we are, we can still do helpful and kindly acts for others. Can *you* think of ways that you can be helpful today?'

Perhaps the teacher could remind the children about those youngsters who received bravery awards at Buckingham Palace. But it is important to stress that small and simple acts of helpfulness are just as important as those seen on TV and that if children make an effort to do the small things in life, they will be ready to do the big things, when the situation occurs.

Prayer

Heavenly Father, Help us to be ready to do a thoughtful deed or a kindly action whenever the opportunity arises. Amen.

Hymn

No. 38, 'Think, think on these things', in *Someone's Singing Lord* (A. and C. Black).

The Enemy Who Became a Friend

This true story from World War II is suitable for older children.

A minister in Burma was preaching about Jesus and helping many people to hide and escape from the Japanese soldiers. One day the minister himself was captured and when he would not give the names of the people who had helped him, he was brutally tortured. Although he was in a great deal of pain, the minister said to his torturer, 'My God has taught me to love my enemies; therefore I forgive you for hurting me.'

After the war was over the minister went back to England and he did not return to Burma for many years. However, one day a group of his old friends wrote to him and invited him back to the small church where he used to preach and from where he had helped so many people during the war. To his great surprise, he came face to face with the torturer of long ago. But what a changed man he saw before him! The man had become a very great Christian, who was helping many, many people. He had become a minister himself and the church was filled with people who wanted to learn more about God.

When the minister from England recognized the Japanese minister, he hugged him and rejoiced with him about all the wonderful things that were taking place. When they were alone together, the minister from England asked, 'But why did you become a Christian?' The Japanese minister said, 'But surely, *you* know. After the war, I couldn't forgive myself for all the terrible things that I had done. I couldn't ask forgiveness of the people that I had hurt, as many were dead or missing. One day I came across this small church — your church — and I found a people here who were so loving and forgiving. They took me into their homes and told me about how Jesus could forgive wrongs, however bad. At last I found peace and happiness and I began to study the Bible. Then I was baptised and confirmed and now I am a Minister.'

Prayer

Heavenly Father, We thank you that Jesus taught us how to forgive others. Help us to be forgiving too. Amen.

Hymn

No. 51, 'The Lord's Prayer', in *Come and Praise*, comp. by G. Marshall-Taylor, arranged by D. Coombes (BBC).

Study of a Neighbourhood

Many fiction books can be read in an assembly to provide a starting point for bringing a topic sharply into focus. Two such books, which show whole neighbourhoods pulling together in the face of disaster, are: Otto S. Svend, *Children of the Yangtze River*, trans. by Joan Tate (Pelham Books, 1982) and Shirley Hughes, *Alfie Gets in First* (Bodley Head, 1981).

Children of the Yangtze River is a lovely story about children who are made homeless by a flood. They re-build their homes and everyone lends a helping hand. This story has proved to be a good discussion starter, particularly for children who have been made homeless for one reason or another. Children can come to terms with disaster when they see how others cope and come to the rescue. The story can also be used to discuss ways in which children in school can collect funds for disaster areas, such as Ethiopia or Armenia.

The second story, *Alfie Gets in First*, shows neighbourhood concern and cooperation, when Alfie races home, shuts himself (and his mother's keys) indoors and he cannot get out or let his mother in. First Mrs MacNally tries to help, then Mrs MacNally's Maureen, then the milkman and the window cleaner, all conspire to set him free; but Alfie solves the problem himself by fetching his chair, standing on it and lifting the catch to open the door. Mum repays the neighbourly kindness by inviting everyone in for a cup of tea. This delightful story can be read to the very youngest children to make them aware of how kind neighbours can be.

The assembly could be concluded by asking the children to take a closer look at their neighbourhood and write down a list of ways that they could be more helpful. Examples could include picking up litter, saying a friendly 'hello' to the next-door neighbour, postman, dustman or milkman. Older children could be asked to consider, 'Who is my neighbour?', not necessarily in the vicinity of their home. Examples could include the lady who drops her purse at the supermarket, the child who is lost, disaster areas at home and abroad. What would each child do? Who would be considered the neighbour in each case?

Prayer

Father, We thank you for good neighbours. Show us how we can be neighbourly ourselves. Help us not to miss opportunities to be helpful and caring today. Amen.

Hymn

No. 37, 'Working together', in *Every Colour under the Sun* (Ward Lock Educational).

5-11
Assembly

A Friend of the Friendless: The Story of Zacchaeus

This is a story of a man who was hated by everyone, who lied and cheated his way through life. As mentioned on pp. 37 and 47, it is beautifully re-told by Roy Castle on one of the Luke Street filmstrips, published by Scripture Union, 130 City Road, London EC1V 2NJ. The filmstrip is for use with the whole school.

The story is called 'The Cheat's House' and shows Zacchaeus as a small fat man. He is swept along by the crowds who wanted to see Jesus. Being so small, he could not see anything. He tried crawling through people's legs, jumping up and down to try and see over their heads, but all to no avail. Suddenly, he had a bright idea and climbed up a tree. When Jesus passed by, he asked Zacchaeus if He could come to Zacchaeus' own home. Zacchaeus felt ten feet tall. No one had ever come to his house before. No one wanted to be his friend. But Jesus and Zacchaeus talked, and Jesus became his friend. Everyone was amazed. The story ends with a chorus of villagers shouting, 'Good old Zacchaeus', 'good old Zacchaeus', as Zacchaeus promises to give back all the money he has stolen.

There are many other lovely stories on the filmstrip including the 'Crowded House', the story of four friends who carried their sick friend to Jesus to be healed. Accompanying the filmstrips are books, picture books to colour and suggestions for activities.

Song

Sing the chorus, 'Zacchaeus was a very little man',

'Zacchaeus was a very little man,
And a very little man was he.
He climbed up into a sycamore tree,
For the Saviour he wanted to see.
And when the Saviour passed that way,
He looked into the tree,
And said, 'Now Zacchaeus, you come down
For I'm coming to your house for tea.'
                                        Anon.

Prayer

Lord Jesus, You have shown us, by your example, how you reached out to a man who had no friends. Help us to reach out to all people today, especially the lonely and friendless. Amen.

Hymn

No. 32, 'Who's that sitting in the sycamore tree?', in *Someone's Singing Lord* (A. and C. Black).

The Case for Team Spirit: Sports Day

At the time of the year when schools hold their sports days, it is especially hard for infants to understand the meaning of winning and losing and the need for team spirit. Indeed, many infant schools question the need for infants to compete at all. But if you are at a school where infants are expected to compete, you may find the following assembly helpful, and it will enable even the youngest child to see that winning or losing does not matter; what really matters is trying one's best.

The whole school should go out of the hall and sit on the grass or playground (weather permitting). Ask the teachers beforehand if they will participate in two races, one a dressing-up race, the other a two-team race, passing a ball over their heads.

Prime various teachers to run the wrong way; get stuck on the starting line; be unable to put on the pyjamas in the dressing-up race; trip before the finishing line; finish the race. Be prepared to give everyone a 'well tried' badge after the race. The second race should be run in two small teams, passing balls over heads.

After the races everyone can either return to the hall or remain seated. Various points should be drawn out:

1 Teacher *X* fell over, but she did not cry; she picked herself up and finished the race.
2 Teacher *Y* couldn't get her dressing-up clothes on, but at least she had a go.
3 Teacher *Z* ran the wrong way but luckily the headteacher helped her to go the right way.

In the team races make sure that everyone sees the significance of taking part. Everyone matters; winners and losers get a badge for effort.

This example may not stop the misery of coming last when you are only 5, but at least it gives each child an example to follow.

Prayer

Lord Jesus, You understand more than anyone that we can't all be winners. Help us to lose gracefully and to realize that it is more important to try one's best than to win. Amen.

Hymn

No. 48, 'Do your best', in *Every Colour under the Sun* (Ward Lock Educational) or No. 57, 'Ready, steady, off we go', in *Sing a Song of Celebration* (Holt, Rinehart and Winston).

The Good Me and the Bad Me

Each child will need:

One piece of card to make a round face
  (both sides will be used)
One piece of paper (with space for five to ten statements on each side;
  less space will be needed for younger children)
Pencil or pen to write with
Felt-tip pens and collage materials to make the face.

Make a model for demonstration purposes:

i.e. a round smiling face on one side of the piece of cardboard

a sad, unhappy face on the other side.

Then attach a piece of paper to the face and ask the children to write down five to ten ideas about what being a good friend means to them. On the reverse side the children should be asked to write in an entirely honest way about ways in which they have been a bad friend.

The faces can be decorated with felt-tip pens, wool, string or material for the hair, etc. Select a number of children to read first the good side and then the bad side of friendship to the rest of the school. End with a short prayer of thanks for all our friends.

Hymn

No. 43, 'Stick on a smile', in *Every Colour under the Sun*, (Ward Lock Educational).

4 People Who Help Us

7–9
Activity

People Who Help Us: Discussion and Activities

There is a need to help children to an awareness of the dignity of man, to respect all people, regardless of age, race, colour or creed. It is sometimes easier to give this respect to those in authority, but children need to see that *all* people should be respected and thanked for whatever job they do, however seemingly menial the task.

This gratitude can be expressed by a simple 'thank you', or the children could be encouraged to write letters of thanks or to draw pictures for those who help in and around the school. Learning to be polite and considerate to visitors, holding doors open for others, considering others before themselves are all ways of achieving this aim.

Discussion Points

1 Talk about the people who work in the school for the common good — caretaker, cook, kitchen assistants, cleaners, secretary, ancillary workers, mothers and fathers, children, teachers, head-teacher, school crossing control person.

2 Then think about the people who come into school from the world outside — school nurse, doctor, dentist, police liaison officer, groundsmen and women, school governors, postmen and women, refuse collectors, school maintenance people like builders, painters, carpenters.

3 Then think about those who help in the community — shop-keepers, hospital employees, bus-drivers, etc. Emphasize that these people are all *friends* of the school, who work for the good of the school community.

4 Talk about school rules. What are they for? Can they ever be broken?

5 Think about how the school community can reach out to other communities. This will be developed in Part 5.

Follow-up Activities for Children

Written Work

1 Make a book about all those people who help in school. Perhaps this could be presented as a 'This is your life' school assembly, when members of the school community are invited to attend.
2 Carry out research on the history of the school. Ask if you can read the old log-books. Perhaps print a school magazine containing 'then and now' extracts and including photo (see *A Record of School Life* on p. 73).
3 Write about 'What I shall remember when I leave my school' or perhaps 'My first day at school'.
4 Describe a part of the school building — the headteacher's room or the kitchen.
5 Interview a member of staff. Think out the questions carefully before you start.
6 Fill a 'time capsule' canister with 'best' pieces of work and a list of all those people who work in the school at present. Ask the headteacher and governors to contribute or include some notices or photographs about school events such as football matches or school choir occasions. This could be buried with ceremony, to be opened in twenty years' time. Don't forget to leave a map!

Religious and Moral Education

1 Find out about what a Jewish school was like at the time of Jesus.
2 There are many stories of how Jesus helped others:
   (i) The woman with the bent back (Luke 13: 10–15);
   (ii) the centurion's servant (Matthew 8: 5–13);
   (iii) Jairus' daughter (Luke 5: 21–42).
3 Do a study of children of the different faith communities who attend your school or live in the neighbourhood. Invite parents into school to talk about special clothes, food, places of worship and the way different faith communities contribute to the richness of the school community. There are many useful books to help with this information: M. Aggarwal and C. Fairclough, *I am a Muslim* (Franklin Watts) 1984, also the following published by Franklin Watts: *I am a Hindu, I am a Sikh, I am a Jew, I am a Rastafarian*, also K. Makinnon, *The Phoenix Bird Chinese Take-Away* London (A. and C. Black, 1978) (about a Chinese family).

Music

Hymn No. 9, 'To God who makes all lovely things', in *Someone's Singing Lord* (A. and C. Black) or No. 3 in *Morning Has Broken* (Schofield and Sims, 1973).

Art/Craft

1 Paint a picture of all those who help in the school.
2 Take each faith in turn and paint parents and children wearing their traditional costumes.
3 Paint pictures of what children used to wear to school in the 1880s in England.
4 Set up a display of Victorian objects. Can your local museum service help you?

Books

CLARKE, B. *Policewoman* (Franklin Watts, 1984).
COOKE, J. *Shops* (Wayland, 1986).
CORBRIDGE, F. *The Ambulance Service* (Wayland, 1985).
ENTICKNAP, J. *The Cook* (Macmillan, 1977).
LANGLEY, A. *Supermarket* (Franklin Watts, 1985, reprint).
LEE, V. *My Class Visits a Park* (Franklin Watts, 1985) intended for 6–7-year-olds; there are some good photographs of travel on the bus and underground in order to get to the park.
MARTIN, C. *Schools in History* (Wayland, 1984) very clear historical descriptions of all the different types of school — Romans, parish schools, monastery schools, dame schools, charity schools, Sunday schools and 'ragged schools', etc.
PEPPER, S. *Hospital* (Franklin Watts, 1984).
ROSS, A. *Going to School* (A. and C. Black, 1982) an absolute must: photographs and original manuscripts and pictures tell the history of schools, rules and punishments.
Round the World Learning (Save the Children Fund and Macmillan Education, 1981) (beautiful photos of schools in different parts of the world, including Third World countries).
STEWART, A. *The Bus Driver* (Hamish Hamilton, 1986).
STEWART, A. *The Dustman* (Hamish Hamilton, 1984).
STEWART, A. *The Nurse* (Hamish Hamilton, 1984).
STEWART, A. *The Postman* (Hamish Hamilton, 1986).

STEWART, A. *The Shop-keeper* (Hamish Hamilton, 1985).
STEWART, A. *The Teacher* (Hamish Hamilton, 1986) (contains photographs of a multicultural school).

Slides

People Who Help Us' and 'Victorian Life' both available from Philip Green Educational, 112a Alcester Road, Studley, Warwickshire B80 7NR, Tel: (0527) 854711.

A Record of School Life

The stove smoked very much today, the wind being in the West. Mr Wilkins, surgeon from Staplehurst came this afternoon to vaccinate. He complained very much about the stove and thought stoves injurious to the health of the children. Grates, he said, would be better and healthier. . . .

While drawing up a pail of water this morning a hen flew down the well and was drowned. I do heartily wish we had a pump, the labour and inconvenience in getting a supply of water for daily use would thus be avoided and a dangerous place covered over. Elizabeth Jarrett broke the schoolroom window. . . .

School is very full. 131 children on the register and only one monitor to assist me. . . .

Source: Extracts from a log-book kept by the headmaster of a village school in Kent, in 1866. In R. Deadman and A. Razzell, *Awareness 2* (Macmillan, 1977) p. 67.

5–7
Assembly

A Pageant

Prior to this assembly a short letter needs to be sent to all parents to ask for their cooperation in sending their children to school dressed as someone who helps us. It needs to be stressed that the costume does not have to be elaborate, but that a simple headdress and a label would do. A list of suggestions could accompany this letter, to include the following.

At home
Mother
Father
Older brothers and sisters
Grandparents
Neighbours

People who come to school
Doctors
Nurses
Dentists
Health visitors
Police Liaison Officer
Road Safety Officer
Gardener
Fire Officer
Lollipop person

At school
Teacher
Secretary
Caretaker
Ancillary Staff
Cook and kitchen staff

In the community
Milkman or woman
Refuse collector
Postman or Postwoman
Shopkeeper
Bus driver
Fisherman or woman
Miner
Police officer
Fireman or woman
Ambulance driver
Lifeboat person
Farmer
Builder
Road worker

Parents should ensure that their child can describe their chosen occupation (all good for language development) with a view to being interviewed by a BBC type interviewer after an initial procession around the hall.

Prayer

We thank you, Dear God, for all the people who help us each day. Bless and protect each one of them. Amen. Or: 'Helpers', in *An Infant Teacher's Prayer Book* (Blandford Press, p. 34).

Hymn

No. 9, 'To God who makes all lovely things', Verse 5, 'He made the people that I meet', in *Someone's Singing Lord* (A. and C. Black).

5–6
Assembly

A Dustman Dance

The teacher needs to explain that a group or class of children are going to portray being litterbugs and dustmen — but that we must all be litre the dustmen and help to keep our school and countryside tidy.

The litterbugs can do a litterbug dance, throwing balls of paper all over the floor. Dustmen enter with sacks and pick up all the paper.

There are some suitable tracks to dance to on Saint Saëns' 'Carnival of the Animals', or dance to 'Here We Go round the Mulberry Bush'.

Prayer

Thank you God for our dustmen. Help us not to be litterbugs. Remind us to pick up rubbish and to discourage others from throwing litter down and spoiling our countryside. Amen.

Hymn

No. 17 'Milk bottle tops and paper bags', in *Someone's Singing Lord* (A. and C. Black).

A Story of an Ordinary Man Who Helped Others

Take a toy helicopter and ask the children if they recognize what it is. Tell the children the true story that they may have seen on television a year or so ago.

A large plane crashed into the River Potomac in the USA just after take-off. The Air-Sea Rescue helicopter was on the scene within minutes of the accident. The water was freezing and the passengers would die quickly if they were not rescued. An ordinary passer-by, seeing that the people in the water were too frozen and shocked to grasp the lowered ladder, jumped into the water and helped pull the passengers to safety. Three times he saved someone, refusing to be saved himself. When the ladder was lowered a fourth time, the man had disappeared.

Prayer

Father, we cannot do anything as great as the man in the story today, but we can be ready to do little things to help each other. Make us ready today to lend a hand, when we see someone in trouble. For in serving others, we are serving you. Amen.

Hymn

No. 34, 'Would you turn your back?' in *Every Colour under the Sun* (Ward Lock Educational).

5–7
Assembly

Dress up a Child

Using any of the people listed in 'A Pageant' (p. 74), dress up one child and ask the children if they can guess what sort of work the person does.

For a shephard/farmer start by giving the child wellington boots. The rest of the children might be encouraged to think of all the occupations that would need waterproof shoes. Then give a warm hat, large jacket, gloves, shepherd's crook, a pitch-fork, a thistle-dodger, etc., explaining the purpose of each item.

This has endless possibilities: a cook, a caretaker, a policeman, a doctor, a gardener, etc. all could be dressed slowly. Finish with a well-known story about a farmer or shepherd from the Bible, or use the filmstrip on Farms produced by Philip Green, Ltd.

Prayer

'Thank you God for the Farmers' in *Infant Assemblies* (Scripture Union, p. 31).

Hymn

No. 89 'See the farmer', in *New Child Songs* (Denholm House Press).

A Visitor

Depending on the local situation, invite a factory worker, a hedge cutter, a vet, a shopkeeper or a Police Liaison Officer into school to describe his/her work. To extend this theme, many visitors can be invited over a number of weeks.

Assume that a police officer has been invited into school. Encourage the policeman to describe his work, perhaps show a film, allow the children to handle his whistle, truncheon, etc. Officers are only too pleased to talk to young children, and this encourages good relationships. Officers will often bring their 'panda car' into the playground and allow the children to look at the controls and speak to base on the two-way radio; or they may bring in working dogs or police horses. This creates great interest among children, to the extent that children and officers then share a common interest and sense of purpose, and fear on both sides dissipates. The children always want to know how the dogs or horses are getting on when they next meet. A visitor can also stimulate much good art, craft, mathematics and written work. End the assembly with a simple prayer.

Prayer

Heavenly Father, we thank you for the visit made by P.C.—this morning. We ask you to help him in his work. Amen.

Hymn

No. 22, I'm very glad of God, in *Someone's Singing Lord* (A. and C. Black).

5–11
Assembly

A Visit to the Fire/Ambulance Station

Children learn best from real experience. A visit to the Fire Station could be arranged — or even more exciting — invite the Fire Engine to the School.

The children should be encouraged to draw, paint and write about their experience and show their efforts to the whole school during Assembly.

Prayer

Children could write their own prayers thanking God for the Fireman.
or
Prayer for Fireman from *First Assemblies* page 182 (Prayer No. 10) published by Blackwell.
or
Heavenly Father, we thank you today for all firemen everywhere. Be with them in their difficult work and protect each one of them from harm as they rescue people in danger.
Amen.

Hymn

No. 44, 'Thank you' from *Sing it in the Morning* . Published by Nelson.

5   People Who Need Help

7–11
Activity

People Who Need Help: Discussion and Activities

Theme

The aim of these assemblies is to demonstrate that real service in the community usually means some sort of personal sacrifice. Caring for others is not easy and yet it brings its own reward.

Children need to see that if they are to help others, it may mean giving up something that they would really like to do, like watching a favourite TV programme, or forgoing a game with a friend. There is a need to emphasize, too, that the children may not always receive thanks and gratitude for their efforts. Perhaps it would be a good idea to remind the children what Jesus said about helping others. 'Whatever you do unto the least of my brothers you do unto me' (Matthew 25: 40).

Discussion Points

1 Discuss the need to reach *out* to the community. Who is part of our community? Who is my neighbour?
2 Talk about facilities for young, old and handicapped in the locality.
3 Find out about voluntary groups and societies working to help those who live near the school.
4 Talk about neighbouring schools, hospitals, the environment generally. Develop a sense of commitment to caring for others and the environment. Ask the children how they could help others.
5 Let the children role play. How easy or difficult is it to live with an elderly person like gran or granpa. What happens when they want to watch a TV programme when *your* favourite programme is on?
6 Try moving like an old person or a handicapped person. Try understanding the other person's point of view and learn how to be more helpful.

Follow-up Activities for Children

Written Work

1 Write letters to charities that look after children. Perhaps the children could 'adopt' one of these societies and find out what the charity actually does for other children. (See suggestions below. Send a large s.a.e. plus a postal order if material is requested.)
2 Carry out research on Doctor Barnardo. Who was he? What did he do? (See 'Resources' below for useful books.)
3 The sign of the fish $\propto$ was the secret sign of the early Christians to tell each other where they would meet to worship and pray. Find out what the symbols stood for: I = Jesus, X = Christ, Θ God's, Y = Son, Σ = Saviour. (These Greek initials make up the Greek word 'fish'; see also p. 34.) Some good neighbour schemes today put the sign of the fish in their windows if help is needed. Design your own 'good neighbour' scheme.
4 Read 'Adopt a Gran' in *Good Morning Children! Assemblies for Junior and Middle Schools* (E.J. Arnold, 1980). Perhaps this could be the start of some interesting work with elderly people.
5 Make a list of all the things that a person in a wheelchair could do with help, from better architectural designs to people being more helpful.

Religious and Moral Education

1 There are many charities that look after children. Here are some suggestions; there are many others. Many societies provide work-packs, filmstrips, books and posters.
   (i)   Save the Children Fund,
       Mary Datchelor House,
       17 Grove Lane,
       London SE5 8RD.
   (ii) The Children's Society,
       Church of England Children's Society,
       Edward Rudolf House,
       Margery Street,
       London WC1X OJL.
   (iii) The NSPCC,
       1 Riding House Street,
       London W1P 8AA.
Help the children to see ways of caring for others.

2 Tell the story of the Good Samaritan in a modern way, e.g. the 'Parable of the Good Punk Rocker' in P. Burbridge and M. Watts *Time to Act* Hodder and Stoughton Limited 1979 (see also p. 93).
3 Another appropriate story is the one Jesus told about the friend who came to borrow a loaf of bread at midnight. (Read Luke 11: 5–11.) There is a good idea for group involvement in J. Gattis Smith, *Show Me* (Bible Society, 1985).

Hymn

No. 59 'Would you walk by on the other side?' in *Come and Praise* (BBC).

Art/Craft

1 Paint a picture advertizing the need to help the young, the old, the handicapped.
2 Make a sausage dog out of material stuffed with old tights to give to an old person to keep out the draughts.
3 Design ways in which buildings and artefacts could be modified to help a person in a wheelchair or someone who is handicapped.

Resources

Books

AVERY, G. *Mouldy's Orphan* (Puffin, 1978) (a lovely story about a little girl who brings home an orphan — but mum and dad are none too pleased!)
HANKS, G. *A Home for All Children: The Story of Dr Barnardo* (Religious Education Press, 1980) (read the part where Barnardo discovers the children sleeping rough in the East End of London).
PARKER, S. *Oxfam* (Religious and Moral Education Press, 1985).
Help the Aged will supply material to display, work cards and teachers' notes phone 071 253 0253 or write to the Education Department, St. James' Walk, London EC1R 0BE.
There are lots of books about children with *special* needs. It may help to foster an awareness of other children's needs by reading some of the following books:
ALTHEA *I Can't Talk Like You* (Dinosaur Publications, 1982).
ALTHEA *I Use a Wheelchair* (Dinosaur Publications, 1983).

FELTHAM H. and ROBSON, M. *Children's Home* (A. and C. Black, 1986).
SOBOL, H. *My Brother Steven is Retarded* (Gollancz, 1978) (an 11-year-old
   girl's feelings about life with her brother).

Film

Dr Barnardo's: The Changing Need, 19 minute colour film available from Dr
   Barnardo's.

7–11
Assembly

Giving and Sharing

(First broadcast on BBC Radio Programme *Discovery*, 3 December 1987)

Children need to develop an awareness of others being worse off than themselves. They need to see the value of sharing whatever they have. They might like to consider the question of whether it is right that half the world is starving and the other half has too much to eat.

This assembly is designed to consider people in the Third World and perhaps offer children an opportunity to give up some of their time, talents and money to help someone in need.

Much material could be displayed showing the needs of the homeless and hungry in other parts of the world. A scrapbook showing children in need and organizations that help could be made by the children. Many or a few children could act this story. If the whole class participates, the children should be divided into two groups. Two main characters are needed; an English boy and a West African boy. Approximately half the class should stand behind each boy, and as the story develops these children could mime the appropriate actions. Simple labels could be worn to assist with characterization, e.g. mother, father, shopkeeper, school children, West African people. Simple props can be used such as knives, forks, spoons and bowls for mealtimes, a Coca Cola tin, nurse's headdress, knitting needles, newspaper. Spot lighting could be used to highlight the different sides of the stage.

The teacher introduces the activity: 'As young as we are, we can all share what we have with others. The story that we are going to act for you today is about one boy who has too much and another boy who does not have enough.'

> *English boy:* When I woke up this morning, my mum gave me sausages, eggs and beans for breakfast. I didn't want the eggs, so I left them on my plate. [Munches food and pushes plate aside. Mother seen cooking.]

> *West African boy:* I couldn't sleep last night because I felt so hungry and thirsty. There is a drought and the waterhole has dried up, so I couldn't have a drink. [Curls up and tries to sleep. Mother and father sadly shake heads.]

English boy: We had fish fingers, chips and peas for school dinners today. I don't like peas, so I told the dinner lady I didn't want them. [All the children eat their dinners. The dinner lady takes plate away.]

West African boy: Every day we are told to report to a camp, ten miles from our home. I am tired and weary and my feet are sore. When we arrive at the camp there is no food left. [Turns hands, palms upwards, in despair. Long queue of children with empty food bowls trudge up to the nurse, who shakes her head. Then queue sits down.]

English boy: On the way home from school I spent £1.50 on chocolates, crisps, fruit gums and a fizzy drink. [Shopkeeper gives items to boy. Boy drinks from Coca Cola tin.]

West African boy: My father has not got any money. We had some cows, but they died when the drought started. We stand in the queue all day, waiting for a little powdered milk. [Queue lines up again. Nurse starts to give out some food.]

English boy: Tonight we had roast chicken and roast potatoes and I went to bed feeling full and ready for sleep. [Family sits round enjoying evening meal.]

West African boy: I try to go to sleep but I feel cold and hungry. It is now three days since I have eaten any food. [Mother cuddles children for warmth.]

English boy: Princess Anne is on the TV. She is asking us to give some money to help save the children in the Gambia. I don't think I'll bother. The people are so far away and I'm sure the money will never get there. I think I'll watch *Star Trek*. [Sits down and watches TV; Father reads newspaper. Mother does her knitting.]

West African boy: Some lady has promised to try and get us some food. But we are told it will take many weeks, months, even. Many of us will die before then. [The rest of the class lie down quietly.]

English boy: I look around and I see people eating and laughing and growing fat. My Mum's on a diet. [Lots of people eating, drinking, laughing.]

West African boy: I look around and I see crying and dying and sad people.

Teacher: We can't all send our pocket money to help the West African families, but perhaps we can have a collection in school for Save the Children Fund, or a charity that helps children (see below), (or our local Children's Home). Or perhaps we can join a scheme to adopt a West African boy. By sending regular amounts of money to that country we can save one boy from starvation. Let us pray for all people in this country and abroad who do not have enough to eat.

Prayer

Heavenly Father, Help each one of us to be ready to share what we have with our neighbour. We pray especially for all those people who do not have enough to eat and we ask that those who have plenty will be ready to share whatever they have with those who have nothing. Amen.
or Prayer 7, 12 from *First Assemblies* (Blackwell).

Hymn

No. 35, 'When I needed a neighbour', in *Someone's Singing Lord*, (A. and C. Black).

Charities That Help Children

Dr Barnardo's
National Children's Home
Shaftesbury Society
NSPCC
Save the Children Fund
Spastics Society
Bible Lands Society
Christian Aid
Oxfam
Missionary departments of Christian Churches

Giving and Sharing: Discussion and Activities

Discussion Points

1 Discuss the fact that even the very poorest child in this country has more food than the boy in Africa.
2 Talk about the boy who has too much; about wasting food, spending our money on wrong things.
3 Discuss ways in which *we* could help others.
4 Talk about what other people are doing at the moment, e.g. Bob Geldof; the farmer in the Midlands who took all his grain to Africa to feed the starving.

Follow-up Activities for Children

Written Work

1 Cut out pictures from newspapers, magazines, etc. of people worse off than ourselves. Write your own report of the situation.
2 Find examples from books and newspapers of injustice to people who have suffered because of their age, race, religion, colour or disability.
3 If your school is in town see if you can link up with a country school. Perhaps you could become pen-pals, visit each other's schools. Learn what it is like to 'live in one another's shoes'.
4 Make two lists: one of things that you consider to be the bare necessities of life; the other of things you consider to be luxuries. Compare your lists with a friend. Then talk about children who live in Bangladesh, or Somalia: do you think that they have any of your bare necessities? Make a new list.

Religious and Moral Education

1 Read Poem No. 123, 'Hunger' and Poem No. 185, 'Famine' in R. Brandling *Assembly Poems and Prose* (Macmillan, 1977) (reprinted on pp. 86–7).

2   Discuss what it feels like to be hungry. Why not hold a 'hunger lunch' — bread and water — and donate the savings to one of the disaster funds? (Permission from parents would have to be obtained first.)

3   Find out about the staple diet of people in different countries. Set up a display of food with a map of the world behind it and link pieces of string from the food to the country of origin. Send for a 'Food pack' from Save the Children Fund.

4   Find out all about bread, how it is made and its religious significance.

5   Think about those who sleep rough, have no food or shelter throughout the year and the charity in London that provides three meals a day and a roof overhead for seven days over Christmas.

6   Try to walk in Jesus' shoes. What would he have done for the poor, the starving, the lonely.

7   Read the New Testament account of Jesus feeding the five thousand (Luke 9: 10–17).

8   Or when he helped the ten lepers (Luke 17: 11–19).

Music

Hymn No. 34, 'God is Love', in *Come and Praise* (BBC) or Song No. 30, 'Streets of London', in *Every Colour under the Sun* (Ward Lock Educational).

Art/Craft

1   Draw a tramp that can be seen on the streets of London.
2   Knit a square or make a patchwork quilt and, with the whole class, make a blanket/cover that could be sent to children in need.
3   Try baking your own bread.

Resources

BRANDLING, R. *Assembly Poems and Prose* (Macmillan, 1977).
HUGHES, M.E. *The Importance of Bread* (Rupert Hart-Davis, 1966) (ten workcards). Recipes for bread-making.

Filmstrips

Bread (Philip Green Educational).

Poems

123 Hunger

Voice 1 Whose are the voices crying, crying?
Whose are the pitiful pleas we hear?
Whose is the sorrow that finds tongue in weeping?
Whose hopelessness speaks with despair?

Voice 2 Ours are the voices crying, crying;
Ours are the pitiful pleas you hear.
We are the people you hear at our weeping
Ours is the empty cry of despair.

Voice 1 Whose are the faces so drawn with suffering?
Whose are the bodies no more than bones?
Whose are the eyes that are hopeless and lifeless?
Whose are the graves with nameless stones?

Voice 2 Ours are the faces gaunt with starvation.
Ours are the wasted dying frames.
Ours are the hungry eyes of the hopeless,
Ours are the graves with no names.

Voice 1 Why do I hear your cries of starvation?
Why show me hunger I don't wish to see?
Why are your skeleton fingers still reaching
Endlessly, endlessly out to me?

Voice 2 Have we been changed so much by our suffering?
In our extremity aren't we the same?
Brother to brother, we reach out our hands to you
Flesh of one flesh are we, name of one name.

Voice 1 What can I do for you brother, my brother?
How can I help? I am too far away.
Leave it to God, hungry brother, my brother,
Go down on your thin starving knees, and pray.

Voice 2 We have prayed distant brother with fierce
     desperation—
Voice 1 Has God in His Mercy shown what you must do?
Voice 2 He has, brother, answered our earnest entreaties
He has answered our prayers and his answer is
     YOU
     Anon

From *Assembly Poems & Prose*, R. Brandling (Macmillan, 1977).

185 Famine

It was by chance that we were born
To plenty in a land of corn.

For some who were born
     In other lands
Less favoured by
     The weather's hand
It was a very bitter price
They paid for want of wheat and rice.

Nigeria's Northern deserts spread
And leave whole tribes to wait for death.

In Bangladesh the rains spill forth
And flood the plains from South to North.
They isolate the village folk
Who least can bear this heavy yolk.

It was sheer chance where we were born.
Should we not send them of our corn?
Christopher Daniels (aged 12) *in Assembly
Poems and Prose*, R. Brandling. (Macmillan
1977)

Christopher Daniels (aged 12) *in Assembly Poems and Prose*, R. Brandling,
(Macmillan, 1977).

A Story Jesus Told: The Good Samaritan or The Parable of the Good Punk Rocker

(From P. Burbridge and M. Watts *Time to Act* (Hodder and Stoughton, 1979)

The piece is performed by the chorus from which the principal parts emerge when required. The narrator should be one of the chorus and act as its leader. 'Rhythm' indicates the sound of a railway train made by the chorus with their hands slapping their thighs, 'FX' is shorthand for appropriate sound effects and actions. Each group will need to work out for itself the precise cues for the rhythm starting and finishing.

Narrator: A man was on a train from London to York [Rhythm]

Chorus: London to York — London to York — London to York — London to York.

Narrator: And as he sat down to read the newspaper he fell among football fans.

Chorus: [FX. Football chant, clapping rather than singing. Repeat.]

Narrator: Who had just seen their team lose the cup.

Chorus: BOO!! What a load of rubbish! [Sung rather than said.]

Narrator: So they mugged the man and took his wallet and his coat. [Four of the chorus mug the man with stylized blows accompanied by:]

Chorus: OOH-OOH, AAH-AAH, OOH-OOH, AAH-AAH.
            [FX. Football chant:]
You'll never walk again, a-gain.
            [Rhythm]

Narrator: Now on that train there was a vicar.

Chorus: [Singing] A — a — men.

Narrator: Who felt sorry for the man.

Chorus: [FX. Four sniffs]

Narrator: So he hid in the lavatory and said a prayer.

Chorus: SLAM! CLICK! [The sounds are produced, rather than the words being said, but there should be accompanying actions.]
[Rhythm]

Narrator: And also on that train there was a social worker from Camden Town who had wide experience with delinquents.

Voice: I really care about the kids.

Chorus: I really care about the kids.

Narrator: She cared so much about the kids that she went to the buffet and had a coffee.

Chorus: [FX. Gulp]
[Rhythm]

Narrator: Also on the train there was the leader of a punk rock group called 'The Dregs'.

Chorus: [FX. Punk Rock]

Narrator: He was the meanest of the mean no-good guys.

Chorus: [FX. Throwing up, or something else suitably off-putting.]

Narrator: But he stopped the train.

Chorus: [FX. Screech. Hiss.]

Narrator: 'Phoned the ambulance.

Chorus: [FX. 'Phoning, followed by approaching siren.]

Narrator: Gave him twenty quid for a new coat.

Chorus: [Sympathetically] Ahhh!

Narrator: And sent him off to hospital.

Chorus: [FX. Siren fading off.]

Narrator: Now where that man came from there were no punk rockers.

Chorus: [FX. Scandalized uppercrust:] 'eaohh!'

Narrator: But there was a vicar.

Chorus: [Singing] A — a — men.

Narrator: And several social workers.

Chorus: I really care about the kids.

Narrator: But when it came to the crunch.

Chorus: [FX. Loud crunch]

Narrator: Who was that man's real next door neighbour?

Voice: Sir ... sir ... please, sir!

Narrator: Yes, Nigel.

Voice: The one that *did* something for him!

Chorus: Oh yes! The one that *did* something for him!

Narrator: Who showed love, love, love, love, love, love, love.

Chorus: Love, love, love, love, love, love, love.

Narrator: Jesus said:

Chrous: [All pointing to the audience] Go!!

Narrator: And do the same.

Chrous: Love, love, love, love, love, your neighbour! [Hugging each other.] Love, love, love, love, love your neighbour!

Voice: [Plaintively] Sir ... sir ... please, sir?

Narrator: [Patiently] What is it, Nigel?

Voice: Who is my neighbour, sir?

Narrator: Two, three:

Chorus: EVERYBODY!!

Voice: Oh yeah. [He laughs idiotically ...]
[Rhythm. Gradually fading off.]

Prayer

People Who Care' in *First Assemblies* (Blackwell, p. 194, Prayers 2, 6, 10).

Hymn

No. 35, 'When I needed a neighbour were you there?' in *Someone's Singing Lord* (A. and C. Black).

(N.B. Permission for a *public* performance of this sketch should be obtained from P. Burbridge and M. Watts, P.O. Box 223, York YO1 1GW)

5–11
Assembly

True Love

This adaptation of the classic O. Henry story is a lovely story about selflessness. Four main characters are needed to mime the actions as the story is read aloud:

A little old man
A little old woman (with beautiful long hair)
A hairdresser
A jeweller

Some simple props are needed:

A hairbrush
A 'gold' clasp for hair
A ribbon
A scarf (to hide hair 'cut off')
A 'gold' watch
A 'gold' chain
A large pair of scissors
An empty purse
Two pieces of wrapping paper

Before the story begins, the little old couple sit in the centre of the stage; the hairdresser sits on the left with simple props and large scissors; the jeweller sits on the right of the stage with the 'gold' chain and 'gold' clasp.

As the story unfolds the main characters mime the actions. The little old lady brushes her beautiful long hair; the little old man takes out his watch and admires it. The hairdresser makes huge cutting movements as the hair is cut off and later ties the child's real hair up with the aid of a hairnet and scarf. The jeweller holds up the beautiful clip and the gold chain for everyone to see and later sells the presents to the old couple.

The old couple wrap the presents and exchange gifts.

Once upon a time there lived an old man and an old woman. They were very poor and hardly had enough money to buy food. But they loved each other dearly and would do anything for each other. They loved God and had learnt much about His ways.

The little old lady had beautiful long hair which she brushed every day [**brush hair**]. It was her proudest possession. She longed for a bright clip to tie back her hair. She had seen one in a jeweller's shop [**jeweller show clip**], but she knew it was far too expensive, and so she made do with a ribbon [**tie with a ribbon**].

She never told her husband that she wanted the clip so badly, but he knew and understood because he had seen her gazing longingly at the beautiful hair clip in the jeweller's shop.

The little old man owned a beautiful gold watch; it had been given to him by his grandfather [**show watch**]. He loved this watch as it was the most precious thing he owned. Every day he would take it out and look at it. He loved it so because it kept such perfect time. He badly needed a chain to hang it on instead of carrying it about with him [**show chain**]. He had seen one in a jeweller's shop, but he never told his wife. Somehow, she knew and understood, because she loved him so.

Soon it was near Christmas, and the little old man and the little old lady began to think and think about what they could buy each other for Christmas. Sadly, the little old lady looked in her purse, but found she had no money left for presents [**look in purse**]. The little old man looked in his pockets, but alas, they were empty [**turn out pockets**]. Suddenly, the little old lady had a wonderful idea. She knew exactly how she could get some money to buy her husband the very present that he would like best of all.

She knew how she could buy the beautiful gold chain. Often, when she had visited her hairdresser, he had told her that if she ever wanted to sell her hair to make wigs, she could make a great deal of money. So quietly she slipped out of the house without telling her husband and she went to the hairdressers. He tool out an enormous pair of scissors and began to cut off all her lovely hair [**cut hair with scissors**]. The hairdresser gave her the money that she needed to buy her husband the gold chain [**give money**]. She went straight to the jeweller's shop and bought the beautiful gold chain. She hurried home to wrap up the present for her husband [**wrap present**].

In the meantime, the little old man thought and thought about how he could buy the beautiful hair clip for his wife. Suddenly, he had a wonderful idea. If he could sell his beautiful watch, he would get enough money to buy the lovely hair clip for his wife. So he hurried to the jeweller's shop and sold his watch [**give watch to jeweller**]. In return, the jeweller gave him the beautiful hair clip [**jeweller give clip**]. The little old man hurried home to wrap up the present for his wife [**wrap up clip**].

On Christmas morning the little old man and the little old woman could hardly wait to give each other their presents. The little old man gave his present first [**give presents**]. Carefully, she opened the parcel and saw the beautiful clip. She stared down at it and then she showed him what she had done to her hair. She gave the little old man his present, and when he saw it was the beautiful gold chain, he told her that he had sold his precious watch to buy her the clip. The two old people hugged each other and laughed because they knew that each had sold their most precious possession in order to show each other their great love [**all go and sit down**].

7–11
Assembly

The Chess Game

(Based on a story called 'The chess match' in R. Brandling, *Assembly Poems and Prose* (Macmillan, 1977). The following adaptation by E.C. Peirce was broadcast on the BBC Schools' radio programme *Discovery*, 1987.

Darren kicked the tin can between two cars. 'Goal', he shouted. He continued running, kicking imaginary goals, using bits of rubbish that lay scattered along the streets. He no longer noticed the slogans painted on the walls of the flats, or the windows boarded over where the occupants were tired of replacing broken glass.

He continued running until he reached his own block of flats. He used to live on the fourteenth floor. He smiled when he remembered how, as a little lad, he couldn't reach the lift button for Floor 14, so he had to press the button for the sixth floor and walk the rest of the way up. Now he lived on the sixth floor, ever since his mum had told the Council man that she couldn't get three children down the stairs when the lift wasn't working. The Council man had been very sympathetic, but he said there just wasn't another flat available, and they would have to wait; and anyway the bottom flats were reserved for the elderly, those old people who couldn't walk any distance at all.

Suddenly, Darren remembered one old lady in particular, Mrs Mac-Nally. Darren had done a dreadful thing. He had broken into Mrs Mac-Nally's downstairs flat. He had smashed a small kitchen window and had climbed in to see what he could steal. He would never forget what happened next; he crept silently through the kitchen, looking in pots on top of cupboards, opening drawers and doors — but found nothing. It was then that he decided to creep through to the sitting room. The room was badly lit and was freezing cold, he was certain that there was no one there, so he continued to search for anything valuable.

Quite suddenly, a boney finger curled around his throat and Darren found himself looking into an old wizened face.

A cracked, broken voice pierced his eardrums, 'You'll not find anything here lad', and then a cackle of laughter followed. Darren was rooted to the spot. He couldn't move.

'Now I've had a good look at ye face, I'll recognize ye again. So what's it to be eh? — the police — or never do anything like this again, come on lad, speak up.' Darren couldn't move. Suddenly the peal of cackling laughter echoed around the room again, filling Darren with fear.

'Do ye play chess?' came the eerie voice. Darren nodded, 'well sit down then.' Darren found himself sitting opposite a chess board with beautifully carved chess pieces all laid out as if the old lady had been playing with someone else.

In the hour that followed everything else was forgotten, as a battle of skills raged, until the old lady wheezed 'checkmate'. Dareen was beaten.

Darren had never been any good at anything at school. His mum had said that if he didn't mend his ways, he would end up in prison.

He smiled now as he remembered his promise to the old lady. He would never break into another flat again, if she didn't tell the police what he had done. In addition, she would teach him to be better at chess than anyone else at school, if he came once a week to play the game with her. He had contemplated never going near the old woman again, but something drew him back each week.

He knew his game was improving. This week he had been picked for the school team to play against a large primary school down the road. The smile on his face broadened into a deep grin as he remembered how he had beaten all his opponents and was now the school champion. He had never told anyone how he had managed to do so well, and he still went to see Mrs MacNally every week.

She had kept her part of the bargain. Now he was looking forward to tonight's match with her. He pressed the lift button for the sixth floor. The lift doors remained tightly closed. No movement. Broken again. He started to climb the dirty, echoey stairs. He would have his tea first and then go and see Mrs MacNally.

He let himself into the flat, his younger brother and sister were fighting and screaming over which TV programme to watch and his mum was washing up at the sink. 'That you Darren? There's a parcel for you on the table.' 'That's odd', thought Darren, 'it's not my birthday, or Christmas.' He rushed over to the table and saw an old, brown paper parcel tied up with string, with his name on it. He quickly undid the knots and then stared down in astonishment. There lay the beautiful chess pieces that had belonged to the old lady. She had left them for him to keep.

Teacher: Why do you think the old lady gave Darren her most treasured possession, especially after the wicked thing he had done to her? Do you think she had forgiven Darren and enjoyed his company? Do you think that she needed his help? Or did Darren need her help in changing his bad behaviour?

What a pity Darren had to learn how nice the old lady was through doing something so dreadful. Still, we can all make mistakes; it's better to say you're sorry and try to put things right than to stay alone, frightened and isolated or even to continue doing those wicked things.

Ask the children to try this week to put right something, that they have done wrong, or to make someone else's day worthwhile by being thoughtful or kind to a lonely person.

Prayer

Father, Forgive us when we do wrong and help us always to try to put things right. Help us to realize that it is always better to own up, rather than to remain alone and frightened and end up in worse trouble. Amen.

Hymn

No. 36, 'Look out for loneliness', in *Someone's Singing Lord*, (A. and C. Black).

6 Harvest

**5–11
Assembly**

A Loaf of Bread

This harvest thanksgiving service is for all those involved in the production and distribution of bread. (Based on an idea given to the author by Rev. Jennings, Eastbourne.)

Buy a large farmhouse loaf. Cut the top off very carefully so that it can be replaced. Hollow out the centre of the loaf. Put the following miniature toys inside, representing those involved in the processes of breadmaking:

mother
father
supermarket worker or shopkeeper
van driver
factory worker or baker
lorry driver
mill worker
driver of combine harvester
farmer
seed

Show the children the loaf of bread and explain that the aim of the service is to give thanks to all those involved in the production and distribution of bread. Ask the children whom they think that they should thank. Now take the top off the loaf and take out the characters with a brief description of their work. Pause and give thanks for each concerned. Finally, give thanks to God for only He can make a seed and provide the right conditions for the seed to grow.

Hymn

No. 56, 'We plough the fields', in *Infant Praise* (Oxford University Press) or No. 55, 'When the corn is planted', in *Someone's Singing Lord*, (A. and C. Black).

Harvest of Ourselves

This harvest festival presentation progresses from giving the usual harvest festival gifts to the more unusual idea of offering our own talents as our harvest gifts.

Narrator: We are going to praise God for the many different kinds of harvest. We shall present this in music, movement and mime. The first kind of harvest that we thank God for is the *harvest of the land*. Watch the seeds unfurling and growing.

[A group of children slowly unfurl and grow tall. Simple costumes can be worn — green jumpers and tights, perhaps some thin strips of crêpe paper attached to the hands and elbows to represent unfurling leaves. The children uncurl slowly to the sound of tambourines played by a small group of musicians or tape-recorded music can be used.]

Narrator: We thank God for all the men and women who work in the *factories*, processing the food that we eat. Here are some of the machines.

[A group of children move like robots or machines. Robot masks can be worn or different sized cardboard cogs can be attached to ordinary clothing. Tape-record some 'machine' music.]

Narrator: We praise God for the *harvest of the sea*. Watch the fishermen haul in their nets, bringing us fish to eat.

[A fisherman's net could be borrowed, or use a few metres of vegetable netting to depict the fishermen hauling in their catch. Brightly painted paper fish could be attached to the netting. The children could wear oilskins, wellington boots or warm clothing and knitted hats. Musicians could play some 'sea' music, or use the water music from *Carnival of the Animals* by Saint Saëns.

Narrator: *Miners* go deep into the earth to bring us coal to give us warmth and heat and light, as well as many other things that we use daily. Years ago women and children hauled the coal out of the mines.

[A group of children could mime the miners at work. Faces should be made dirty and smudged. Dark clothes, Balaclava hats and a real miner's lamp would help to add authenticity. Xylophones or tape-recorded music could assist the action.]

Narrator: Finally, we are going to show our thanks to God for his rich harvest by offering our own talents, big or small, as our harvest gift.

The children will show either what they can do *now*, or what they would like to do when they *grow up*. [Each child takes his or her turn to mime something useful — putting a caring arm around a child who is crying; carrying a heavy basket of shopping for an old lady; doing the washng up for Mum or Dad; singing in the choir; taking part in the school sports; playing a musical instrument. Appropriate costumes can be worn to depict the particular talent being offered, e.g. leotard for the gymnast. Suitable music could be tape-recorded for each child's action.

Narrator: This is the harvest of our school. We are all working together, so that we can produce a rich harvest of talents.

[The children could make up their own prayers about striving for excellence in all things.]

Prayer

Father God, We thank you for your wonderful harvest gifts to us. We thank you for the harvest of the land, the harvest of the sea, the harvest of the mines, and the harvest from the factories. We offer ourselves to you today, to live and work to your glory. May our school produce a rich harvest of talents. Amen.

Hymn

No. 56, 'The farmer comes to scatter the seed,' in *Someone's Singing Lord* (A. and C. Black).

5–7
Assembly

Harvest of the Hedgerows

If possible, before this assembly, take the children on a nature walk and try to find the following: rosehips, hazelnuts, acorns, haws, bullaces, blackberries. If this is not possible, then set up a large picture display with clear pictures of the above items. (Good pictures can often be found in back issues of *Child Education*.) If you are able to provide both the pictures and the items, link each item with a piece of tape to the picture displayed behind the table. Give the children the following information:

Rosehips: These come from the wild rose. They can be gathered and made into a drink and birds eat them.

Hazelnuts: These come from the hazel tree. They are very nice to eat. Squirrels collect them and store them for winter, and birds, like the Nuthatch, eat them. It is very surprising that these tiny birds are able to crack open the nuts by hammering with their strong beaks on the shells to get the kernels out.

Acorns: These come from the oak tree. Squirrels and mice store them. Pigs and pigeons love them. Did you know that during World War II children collected acorns and sent them to London Zoo to feed to the animals when food was short?

Haws: These come from the hawthorn bush. Birds eat them. Haws stay on the trees for most of the winter, so birds have their own special food.

Bullaces: These are a type of wild plum. They are delicious to eat. Birds love them. They can also be made into wine or jam.

Blackberries: Birds and mice and insects feed on these as well as people. They can be eaten fresh or put into pies or made into jam.

Prayer

End the assembly with a simple prayer of thanks to God for providing food for the birds, insects and animals in the autumn.

Hymn

No. 3, 'Harvest, harvest come along,' in *Every Colour under the Sun* (Ward Lock Educational).

5–9
Activity/Assembly

Animals and Insects Giving for Our Harvest

Choose four or five animals or insects to study in depth, e.g. sheep, cows, chickens, goats, bees. Classbooks, pictures, posters, real life examples (if possible) can be gathered together to form the final assembly after many weeks of careful study and preparation. Each animal could form the basis of one assembly before the finale when all the work is shown. Take each animal in turn and find out as much as possible.

SHEEP

Write to the British Wool Marketing Board, Oak Mills, Station Road, Clayton, Bradford, West Yorkshire B14 6JD for information on the different breeds of sheep. If possible, invite a farmer to bring a sheep into school. Collect some sheep's wool from fences around fields; or try to purchase a part of a fleece. Ask the children to make a list and paint or draw all the things that are made of wool. If possible, try to dye some wool using natural dyes like beetroot or other vegetables. Try to find pictures of old spinning wheels. If you know someone who can spin, invite them into school or perhaps visit a mill. Make a classbook about all the things you have learnt about sheep (See page 175 for a story about sheep.)

Let each child tell the whole school something that they have learnt about sheep; or let the children hold up their pictures or experiments with wool; or invite the farmer into school to talk about the sheep's year from lambing to shearing. (see story on p. 174).

Resource

CLAXTON, J. and DOGARIS, S. *Three Bags Full* (Hamish Hamilton, 1976).
MOON, C. *Sheep on the Farm* (Wayland, 1983).
Charts are available from the British Wool Marketing Board (see above).

Prayer

Heavenly Father, Thank you for the different kinds of sheep that provide wool to keep us warm in winter time. Amen.

Hymn

No. 48, 'The Lord's my Shepherd', in *Come and Praise* (BBC).

COWS

Milk, cream, butter and cheese all come from cows. Find out about the different breeds of cows. What do they eat? Find out how cows are milked. How many pints could one cow produce in her lactation period? (Answer: 24,000 pints). How is milk measured? What happens to the milk at the dairy? Find out about the different uses for milk: cream, butter, skimmed milk, yoghurt, cheese, etc. Conduct research on old-fashioned milk pails, shoulder yokes and churns. Learn about George Barham who in 1566 became the first man to start a dairy company in London. Make a map of England and put a flag on the spot where these cheeses come from: Wensleydale, Lancashire, English Cheshire, Derby, Leicester, Stilton, Caerphilly, Double Gloucester, English Cheddar. Try to find out about cheeses from around the world.

Resources

LANGLEY, V. *Dairy Produce* Hove, (Wayland 1981).
PATTERSON, G. *Dairy Farming* (Andre Deutsch 1983).
PITT, V. *A First Look at Cheese* (Franklin Watts 1982).
WHITLOCK, R. *Dairy Cows* Hove, (Wayland 1982).

The National Dairy Council Education Department, John Princes Street, London W1M OAP (Tel.: 071 499 7822) provides many educational aids, wall charts, etc. Much of this material is distributed free of charge.

Prayer

Thank you Father for the cows who give us so much. We thank you for fresh milk, and different cheeses, yoghurt, cream and butter. Thank you Heavenly Father, for these gifts. Amen.

Hymn

No. 53, Verse 3, 'The cows and sheep in the meadows,' of 'The flowers that grow in the garden,' in *Someone's Singing Lord*. (A. and C. Black).

CHICKENS

If possible, set up an incubator in the classroom and hatch your own chickens. It takes twenty-one days at carefully controled temperature and turning the eggs three times a day. Children will learn far more from real experience. Find out about different breeds of chicken. Make a list of as many ways as possible that we use or eat eggs. Make a large diagram of what an egg looks like inside. Show the children how to test whether an egg is fresh or not. Try some egg recipes; perhaps make some meringues. Find out about grading eggs. What is meant by large, standard, medium, small? Is there any difference between brown and white eggs? Try decorating hardboiled/blown eggs. Make an egg-shell collage. Explain how some broody chickens make very good foster-mothers and can hatch out ducks or geese, as well as chicks. Try and visit a farm and take note of any rare breeds.

Resources

HINDS, L. *Eggs* (Franklin Watts 1982).
WHITLOCK, R. *Poultry* (Wayland 1982) Chart is available from Poultry
    World, Surrey House, Throwley Way, Sutton, Surrey SM1 4QQ
    (Tel.: 081 643 8040).

Prayer

Loving Father, we thank you for your gift of eggs; for the variety of ways in which this harvest gift can be used in cooking. Make us mindful of those who do not have enough to eat. Amen.

Hymn

No. 2, 'The golden cockerel', in *Someone's Singing Lord* (A. and C. Black).

HONEYBEES

How can honey be used? We can eat it on bread; use it as a substitute for sugar; use it as an antiseptic for cuts; use it to soothe sore throats and coughs; put it in cakes; make honey drinks. Find out all you can about bee-keeping, hives, queens, drones, workers, eggs, larvae and pupae. How can beeswax be used? Make large-scale drawings of the queen, workers and drones. Learn about the honeybee's dance — the 'round dance', and the 'waggle-tail dance'. Perhaps the children could make bee head-dresses and show the rest of the school some of the 'bee dances'. How much honey could we expect from one hive (Answer: approx. 33–44 lbs.). Find out how many different coloured honeys there are. Why are they a different colour? Why not set up a small observation hive in the school?

Tell the Aesop tale, 'Jupiter and the Bee'. It is a cautionary tale about how the queen bee gets her sting, which if used to sting others, will cause her to die herself. This story is beautifully retold in R. Fisher, *Together with Infants* (Evans Brothers, 1982).

Resources

MUNRO, S. *Honey* (Franklin Watts Reprint, 1982).
SINCLAIR, W. *Life of the Honeybee*, a Ladybird Natural History book, (Wills and Hepworth Ltd., 1969).
Child Education Special, (Scholastic Publications Ltd., April 1986).

Prayer

Heavenly Father, We thank you that such a little tiny insect can provide us with such a rich harvest. Amen.

Hymn

No. 42, 'I love God's tiny creatures', in *Someone's Singing Lord*, (A. and C Black).

From a Seed to a Chair

The following props are required for this assembly:

infant wooden chair (or antique chair)
display of carpenter's tools
children's display of wooden toys
acorn
oak seedling

The assembly could be developed over several days. Start with the chair and describe the process from a seed to the finished product (see brief description below). On the second day invite a carpenter into school to describe each tool and its purpose. Link this with Jesus learning the carpenter's trade and discuss what he might have made. Finally, encourage the children to learn about different woods and appreciate their beauty and versatility. Invite the children to bring wooden items or toys from home to set up a 'wooden' display in school. End the series with a general thanksgiving for trees, timber, skill of the craftsmen, useful and beautiful wooden items. Warn them of the dangers of the mindless destruction of trees and the ruination of the rain forests.

As the first day's activity, look at a wooden chair. Have you ever thought where the wood came from and who made it? One of our most treasured timbers comes from the oak tree, which can grow to the height of 100 feet. However, the oak tree begins its life like this [show acorn]. It grows from a tiny seed. It takes many, many years for an oak tree to grow to the size necessary for cutting down and making into timber for carving by a craftsman. When it has reached maturity, the tree is cut down and sent to the sawmill, where it is cut into smaller pieces of timber. Then it is stacked and allowed to dry for a very long time, otherwise it would twist and warp and be useless. Finally, it can be used by the carpenter, the craftsman who has the tools and the skills to shape the wood (show carpenter's tools). Once the shapes have been made, the carpenter fits all the pieces together with great care and makes a thing of beauty that will last for years and years.

Perhaps the children could try to find out which is the oldest known chair in England, or make a scrapbook depicting different types of chairs, or visit a museum to find out about the various woods from which chairs have been made, or visit a modern furniture factory.

Prayers

Father, We thank you for the wonder and beauty of trees. For the miracle of growth from a tiny seed to a tree such as the mighty oak. May we be preservers of trees, not destroyers. May we each play our part in planting trees for the future. We thank you for the many things that come from wood and the skill of the craftsmen, who shape the wood for our use. Amen.
Or 'The Prayer of the Tree'.

The Prayer of the Tree

You who pass by and would
raise your hand against me,
hearken ere you harm me,
I am the heat of your hearth
on the cold winter night,
the friendly shade screening
you from summer sun,
And my fruits are refreshing
draughts quenching your thirst
as you journey on.
I am the beam that holds your house,
the board of your table,
the bed on which you lie,
the timber that builds your boat,
I am the handle of your hoe,
the door of your homestead,
the wood of your cradle,
the shell of your last resting place.
I am the gift of God and the friend of man.
You who pass by, listen to my prayer,
Harm me not.

Anon.

Hymn

No. 18, 'Give to us eyes', in *Someone's Singing Lord* (A. and C. Black).

A Harvest Tea at School

Jsing some of the recipes shown below, the children could make flapjacks, lackberry and apple pies, pineapple upside-down cakes, oatmeal biscuits, hortbread, scones, etc. and invite some local people in for a special harvest ea. With help, the children could serve the food that they have made.

The afternoon could be drawn to a close by singing some well-known arvest songs and saying some prayers made up by the children, or use the ollowing prayer.

Prayer

Thank you God, for this lovely food and for the fun we have had in naking it. Amen.

Hymn

No. 3, 'Harvest, harvest come along', in *Every Colour under the Sun* (Ward ock Educational) or No. 56, 'We plough the fields and scatter the good eed on the land', in *Infant Praise* (Oxford University Press).

Flap Jack Recipe

ou will need:
oz/75 g margarine
oz/75 g brown sugar
oz/100 g oats
Pinch of salt

Method:
Set the oven at 350°F/180°C.
Warm margarine.
Mix sugar, oats, salt into margarine.
Flatten mixture into a baking tray. Smooth the surface with a knife.
Place tray in oven for 20 mins.
After cooking cut into squares.

Shortbread Recipe

You will need:
2 oz/50 g caster sugar
4 oz/100 g margarine
6 oz/150 g self-raising flour

Method:
1   Set the oven at 325°F/165°C.
2   Rub margarine into the flour.
3   Stir in sugar.
4   Grease baking tray and press mixture onto the tray.
5   Bake for 20 mins.
6   Cut into squares.

5–11
Assembly

Sharing Our Harvest Gifts: A Bowl of Rice

Adapted from a lesson in M. Ashby (Ed.) *R.E. Handbook: A Resource for Primary School Teachers* (Scripture Union, 1983) (by permission of Scripture Union).

The following props are required for this activity talk.

A bowl of cooked cold rice
Spoon
Nine plates
Selection of appetizing harvest gifts such as tin of spaghetti, ham, macaroni cheese, etc.

Choose nine children to come and stand out at the front in a line. Give each child a plate. Give every third child a spoonful of rice. Ask for the children's comments. Do you think that is fair? What about those who haven't got anything? Go back down the line and give those children who had nothing as many tins of good food as can be fitted on their plates. Ask the children if it is fair now? Explain to the children that two-thirds of the world have good things to eat, while one-third has only very little.

Ask the children in the line who have the good things what they should do with their food to make it more fair for those children with only some rice. Let the children share out their tins with each other. Look carefully at how the children decide what to keep and what to give away. Comment if necessary. Finally, explain how the harvest gifts will be distributed to those who do not have very much.

Prayer

Father, you have made us deeply conscious of those who do not have enough to eat. Help us always to be generous. Amen.

Hymn

No. 31, 'Because you care', in *Every Colour under the Sun* (Ward Lock).

7–11
Assembly

Preserving Our Harvest Gifts: A Tin of Fish

The following props are required for this activity:

Selection of tinned fish — tuna, pilchards, mackerel
Chart of different fish (published by Macmillan)
Children's own fish pictures
Fish mobiles (ideas in Michael Grater's *One Piece of Paper* (Mills and
   Boon, 1963)

Begin with the tins of fish. Ask various questions to elicit knowledge: Who knows what they are? Have you ever eaten this kind of fish? What is your favourite fish? How does the fish get into the tin? Are *tins* of fish caught?

Outline brief history of the tin. The story goes back to 1795 in France. The French government had a huge army and navy and the troops all needed to be fed. The government offered a great reward to anyone who could invent a method of preserving food so that it would remain fresh enough to be sent to the troops.

For fourteen years the prize remained unclaimed, then a sweet-maker called Nicholas Appert used a wide-mouthed glass jar to preserve some food. He placed the food inside the jar, heated it to drive out the air, which he thought was the cause of food deterioration, and then he fitted the top with a cork to keep the contents fresh. Soon he supplied the troops with plenty of bottled meat, fruit and vegetables. In 1809 he collected the prize from Napoleon himself.

The following year an Englishman named Peter Durand used a metal canister based on the design of an old tea canister. Hence the word 'can'.

In those early days cans had to be made by hand, which was a very slow and costly process, and there were many problems. The tins kept bursting and the food often went bad. It wasn't until 1857 that Louis Pasteur discovered that it was not air that destroyed the food, but minute organisms called bacteria.

Today these problems have been overcome and many millions of cans of food are made every day, preserving the food as fresh as the day it was brought to the canning factory.

It is because of the tin can that we are able to send food quickly to disaster areas in the world, to prevent people from starving. Parcels of tins can be dropped by aeroplane where food is needed.

We can give tins of food to old or sick people who cannot get out to buy food for themselves. We know the tinned food will be just as good.

Perhaps schools could request a 'tin only' harvest festival for delivery to local old people in need.

Prayer

Thank you, Lord, for the exciting world of tins, for the variety of food that is kept quite fresh and tasty for long periods. As we give our tins away today, to people in need, we ask you to bless each one of them and us. Amen.

Hymn

No. 36, 'God is love', in *Come and Praise* (BBC).

7   Festivals

**5–11
Assembly**

Carnival before Lent

Before this carnival assembly, the children need to know something about the importance of Lent in the Christian calendar. Lent today is remembered as the forty days before Easter, when Jesus went into the desert and was tempted by the devil. (see Matthew 4: 1–11). Jesus went without food during this period, and three times the devil tempted Jesus with riches rather than sacrifice. But Jesus rejected the devil. Christians try to follow in Jesus' footsteps and go without something that they particularly like during Lent, giving the money saved to charities.

Ash Wednesday marks the beginning of Lent, but is immediately preceded by Shrove Tuesday. 'Shrove' comes from the word 'shriven', which means to be forgiven. Christian people traditionally ask God's forgiveness on this day for all the things that they have done wrong. Shrove Tuesday is also known as 'Pancake Day', because people used to use up all their luxury foods like fats and sweet things, making pancakes before they gave those foods up during Lent. Ash Wednesday is so called because Christians used to mark their foreheads with ashes to show their repentance for their sins. Some Christians still do this today.

Other Christians, like many in the Caribbean, hold a carnival before Lent before the strict self-denial that Lent brings. People dance to beautiful steel bands and calypso music, a carnival king and queen are chosen and people wear fantastic costumes. All sorts of themes for the costumes can be chosen, such as beautiful flowers, birds, fish, animals.

For this assembly children could have great fun making masks and head-dresses and hold a carnival dance. But a simpler assembly could be arranged by playing some good steel band music and allowing each class to dance in turn. (Warn them beforehand that when the music stops, they must return to their places.)

Prayer

Father God, help us to be generous in our giving, not only during Lent, but all through the year. Amen.

Hymn

No. 64, 'Everybody loves carnival night', in *Tinder-Box: 66 Songs for Children* (A. and C. Black).

**5–11
Assembly**

Easter: The Ugly Man

Explaining the meaning of Easter to 5-year-old children is exceedingly difficult. I have told the story first as it is in the New Testament, spending each day of a week talking about the events that led to the death of Jesus (see Luke chapters 22–24). But I was always left wondering if the children really understood the story, particularly why any man should want to give his life for others.

The story of the ugly man solves this problem and helps explain why a man should wish to die for someone else. It is based on a story called 'He Died for Us' by Dee Moss in *Today's Talks for Today's Children* (Chester House Publications, 1967). Having told the story for many years to infant children, I adapted it for the BBC Radio Programme *Discovery* in 1987 for 7–9-year-olds. (See also Part 8, 'Celebration of New Life after Death', p. 144).

Gary was very excited. After school he was going to meet an uncle that he had never seen before. He wasn't a real uncle, but someone his mum and dad had known for a very long time and they called him 'uncle'. He knew all *about* his 'uncle', because every Christmas and birthday he had received fantastic toys from him, as well as long amusing letters throughout the year, since he had been a very small child.

Gary's parents were always talking about Gary's uncle — what fun they used to have with him when Gary was a baby; they talked about his uncle's marvellous sense of humour and his great love of life. So Gary couldn't *wait* to meet him. The day at school seemed to drag on forever as he struggled with his French and then his mathematics, and all the other subjects. At last the bell went. Gary raced out of school, to start the long walk home. A group of Gary's friends took the same route home, and they always walked together, laughing and joking along the way. But this time something happened, something that had never happened before. Ahead of the children was an old, bent crippled man with a burnt, scarred face. The scars were livid red and twisted and contorted the man's face. Along the man's arms and neck and hands more lumps and scars could be seen. Part of the man's hands had been eaten away. The man looked *so* ugly.

'Scar-face', shouted one of the boys. 'Uagghh, isn't he ugly', shouted another. 'Look at his hair — he looks as if he's seen a ghost.' Then one of the boys did a most despicable thing, he picked up a stick and started poking the man, and another boy pulled the man round in circles, ripping the man's coat. Gary, led on by the others, began to shout rude names and to jeer and to laugh. When they had had their 'fun', they left the poor man hobbling along the road, and they continued to shout rude names over their shoulders, as they raced home until they were out of sight.

Gary ran on home, pushed open the garden gate, called out to his mum that he was home and rushed upstairs to change out of his school uniform. Just then, he heard the garden gate click and so he rushed to the window to catch a first glimpse of his uncle. Oh no, who do you think was coming up the garden path? None other than the bent, scarred man that he had taunted on his way home. Gary felt devastated, surely this man couldn't be *his* uncle, *surely* there was some mistake. But his mother's call confirmed that his uncle had arrived, and told him that this was no mistake.

'I've got to hide', Gary whispered, 'I can't possibly meet him. He will recognize me. Oh, what have I done?' Gary's mother continued to call, and eventually she came upstairs to get him. White as a sheet, Gary went downstairs and was introduced.

If the scarred man recognized Gary as one of the rude boys who had ill-treated him, he never said, and as they talked and Gary's uncle began to tell some of his exciting stories over tea, Gary soon forgot about the terrible scars and his own terrible behaviour earlier.

Soon it was time for Gary's uncle to leave, and Gary felt very sad because he knew this man was truly a great man. When Gary's dad came to say good-night that night, Gary said, 'Dad, how did my uncle get those terrible scars on his face, arms and hands? You never mentioned them to me before.' Gary's dad said, 'Well, your uncle never talks about it, but when your mum and I were much younger, we went on holiday. We stayed in a caravan. We took our tiny baby with us. It was such a lovely evening that first night, so we just stepped outside the caravan for a few minutes and we were talking to some other people who were staying on the same camp site. Suddenly, we heard someone yelling 'fire! fire!' We turned round and saw that our caravan was on fire. The fire spread quickly throughout the caravan, thick smoke and flames came pouring out the windows and doors. Your mum screamed, 'Our baby is in there.' We began running, other people began running and yelling, 'Go back, go back. You will be burnt.'

Ahead of us, a young man ran out of the crowd and into the flaming van. Seconds later he re-emerged, like a flaming torch, his arms, hair and clothes were all on fire, but he was using his body to shield something, to shield our tiny baby. Our baby was unhurt, but the man was badly burnt and he was rushed to hospital. He stayed in hospital for many months while surgeons fought to save his life and rebuild his burnt body using plastic surgery. 'That's when we became very great friends, because you see we were so grateful to him.'

Gary was silent. Then he whispered, 'That baby was me wasn't it, and that man is now the man I call 'uncle'. His bravery saved my life. His courage cost him his good looks. He was turned into an ugly man for my sake, and I have hurt him.' Gary turned away and quietly cried.

Prayer

Dear Lord Jesus, we know, that just like the man in the story, you were hurt for our sakes. Help us to use the new life that we have been given in your service. Amen.

Hymn

No. 51, 'We have a king who rides a donkey', in *Someone's Singing Lord* (A. and C. Black) or No. 69, 'At Easter time', in *New Child Songs* (Denholm House Press).

5–11
Assembly

Ascension Day Picnic

After Jesus' death the disciples were very sad; then came the joy of Jesus' resurrection, three days later. During the next forty days Jesus appeared to many people. (See Part 8, 'Celebration of New Life after Death', p. 144). On one such occasion he had breakfast on the beach with his friends (John 21: 1–14), and you cannot have breakfast with a ghost!

But Jesus told his friends that soon he would have to leave them and return to his Father. This had to happen, so that he could send His Spirit to empower his disciples world-wide. (See following assembly on Whitsunday.) He also promised that he would return.

Luke 24: 45–53 tells us about this, and about Jesus' ascension into heaven. The disciples were not sad that this was to be the last time that they were to see Jesus, but we are told in Luke that the disciples went back to Jerusalem filled with great joy.

Many schools, therefore, use this day as a cause for celebration. What nicer way to celebrate than to plan a picnic, with everybody sharing their meal, space and weather permitting!

Prayer

Lord Jesus Christ, We remember that on this day you returned to your Father, in heaven. Help us to carry on your work, here on earth. Amen.

Hymn

No. 47, 'God who put the stars in space', in *Someone's Singing Lord* (A. and C. Black).

5–11
Assembly

Pentecost or Whitsunday Assembly

Ten days after Jesus' ascension into heaven and fifty days after Jesus' resurrection came Pentecost (the Greek word for fiftieth). Jews celebrated 'Shavout' on this day, or the giving of the law at Mount Sinai, fifty days after their Passover Festival. (See material in Part 14 for further information regarding Pentecostal Christians (see pp. 257–8) and the second volume for Shavout assembly.) This was the day that God sent his Holy Spirit to empower his disciples to preach the gospel to all nations. (The following activity is based on an idea given to the author by Rev. R. Mann, Broadwell.)

Ask for twelve volunteers from the floor to come out and help you. Whisper to these children that they must go back and choose just one person to whisper something that Jesus taught — God loves them, or Jesus is alive — and then go and sit down.

When everyone is quiet, explain to the rest of the children that the twelve volunteers have just become the first missionaries to the school, and that this is how the gospel has spread throughout the ages, with each person telling somebody else the good news, that Jesus broke the power of death and can forgive our sins, and is alive through His Spirit within us.

The name 'Whitsunday', came from the words 'White Sunday' because, as people heard the good news, they wanted to be baptized at Pentecost or Whit-sunday, as an outward sign of turning from their old life to a new life, and a tradition grew up to wear white for the baptism.

In England today there are still some street processions on Whitsunday (e.g. in Manchester), when children wear white to commemorate the first coming of the Holy Spirit.

Prayer

Lord Jesus, We know that your Holy Spirit is available to all who ask. So we ask you to help us now to be more like you. Amen.

Hymn

No. 16, 'For all the strength we have', in *Someone's Singing Lord* (A. and C. Black).

The Twelve Days of Christmas

The problem of how to involve every child in an infant school, with approximately five classes of thirty children per class, in the Christmas production is beautifully solved by dancing, singing and miming to the song 'The Twelve Days of Christmas'. Additional parts can be found for many angels and shepherds, oxen and asses, wise men and pages, plus Mary and Joseph, by simply adding a final verse using the same tune, but with the words:

> But the best gift of Christmas,
> I am sure you will agree
> Is God's gift to everyone
> Of a ti — ny ba — by.

For this activity you will need:

One announcer with scroll containing the words of the song 'The Twelve Days of Christmas'
Two true loves
One partridge
One pear tree
Two turtle doves
Three French hens
Four colly birds
Five gold rings
Six geese a-laying
Seven swans a-swimming
Eight maids a-milking
Nine drummers drumming
Ten pipers piping
Eleven ladies dancing
Twelve Lords a-leaping

(Different versions may vary as to who does what.)
This makes a total of eighty-two children to be involved. To this number approximately sixty-three (or more) further children can take the

parts of the Nativity tableau, making a total of approximately 150. Children to be involved altogether.

Two for Mary and Joseph
Twenty angels
Twenty shepherds
Three wise men
Three page boys
Five oxen
Five asses
Five sheep

The Dramatic Movement

The drama takes place in-the-round. All the children come into the hall and sit in a huge circle, dressed as the different gifts in the order of the song — true loves, partridge, turtle doves, etc. The parents also sit in a circle around and behind the children, so that they can see the whole production. The announcer reads the following: 'On the first day of Christmas my true love sent to me ... [pause]. Here are the two true loves.' Announcer sits down. Two children dressed in huge red hearts sewn onto white shifts stand up and move to the centre of the circle. Popular music is played for a few minutes to which the two children dance. (See below different music for the different dances of the gifts.) The true loves then stand at one end of the circle and the announcer re-appears).

> *Announcer:* On the first day of Christmas my true love sent to me a partridge in a pear tree.

The announcer sits down. A child dressed as a pear tree stands up and walks to the centre of the circle. The child dressed as a partridge also stands up, bows to the true loves and dances to his piece of music, before coming to rest and return to his seat. Both actors then sit down.

The whole operation is repeated, with the announcer announcing each gift, who dances in turn before the true loves, until the final verse of the original song. Then all the children *sing* the original song (encourage the parents to sing as well). As each child hears their part sung, they can stand up and take a bow.

Finally, the children *only* sing the new verse, 'But the best gift of Christmas, I'm sure you will agree, is God's gift to everyone of a tiny baby.' At this point the Nativity pageant stand up, and in turn walk round the circle with dignity, to make a central tableau of Mary, Joseph and Jesus, angels holding their wings high, shepherds kneeling, oxen and asses and sheep crouching around the outer edges of the circle. There are many appropriate Christmas hymns, in *Carol, gaily carol*, (A. and C. Black) which can be sung as each group plays its part.

Then all the children, parents and teachers can be invited to sing 'Silent night', or 'Away in a manger' before Mary and Joseph lead the whole cast quietly out of the hall.

The Music for Dancing

Some well-known classical pieces of music which are also very popular are suitable, e.g. the double album entitled *Classics 100*, published by K-Tel International UK Ltd, 35/37 Sunbeam Road, London NW10. Using the following pieces, the children can mime their parts — pipers piping, drummers drumming, etc. — and improvise their dance to the music.

> *True loves* danced to Mozart, *Piano Concerto No. 21*, 'Elvira Madigan' Theme.
> *Partridge* danced to Tchaikovsky, *Piano Concerto No. 1*.
> *Two turtle doves* danced to Offenbach, 'Barcarolle' from *The Tales of Hoffman*.
> *Three French hens* danced to Ponchielli, Galop from *The Dance of the Hours*.
> *Four colly birds* danced to Tchaikovsky, *Waltz from the Serenade for Strings*.
> *Five gold rings* danced to Boccherini, *Minuet*.
> *Six geese a-laying* danced to Bizet, *March of the Toreadors from Carmen*.
> *Seven swans a-swimming* danced to Chopin, *Prelude in A Flat*.
> *Eight maids a-milking* danced to Chopin, *Grand Waltz from Les Sylphides*.
> *Nine drummers drumming* danced to Chopin, *Military Polonaise*.
> *Ten pipers piping* danced to Schubert, *Marche Militaire*.
> *Eleven ladies dancing* danced to Johann Strauss, *Blue Danube Waltz*.
> *Twelve lords a-leaping* danced to Brahms, *Hungarian Dance No. 5*.

The Costumes

The costumes were of the simplest type, mainly consisting of a simple head-dress, made by a working party of mothers and teachers.

True loves: White sheets cut into shifts for boy and girl, with red hearts sewn on back and front, white tights, one red rose which the boy presents to the girl at the end of the dance, tinsel in the girl's hair.

Partridge: Brown jumper and brown tights, with small bird mask (consisting of yellow beak and black eyes), large wings of cardboard attached from the shoulder to the little finger which loops over the finger.

Pear tree: Green sheet cut into half-moon shape, with golden pears (made out of foil) attached, twig or leaf head-dress.

Turtle doves: White vests or leotards and white tights, with very soft white fabric attached from middle of the back to little finger (to give wing effect), white ballet shoes if possible.

French hens: Red cones attached to a head-band, tunics with feathers (made out of paper).

Colly birds: Bird masks (see M. Grater, *Paper Faces* London (Mills and Boon) 1967), black jumpers and black tights.

Gold rings: Yellow jumpers and yellow tights, with gold bands around heads. Dancing with PE hoops covered in gold foil.

Geese a-laying: Yellow webbed feet made out of cardboard, white shifts drawn together at the throat and just below the knees (can be padded out with soft cushions), hard-boiled eggs to produce at the end of their dance.

Swans a-swimming: Crêpe paper ballet skirts sewn onto a band tied around the waist with white tops and white tights, tiny wings attached to backs.

Maids a-milking: Floral dresses with white aprons and white mob-caps, plastic buckets and three-legged stools if possible.

Drummers drumming: Military uniforms look very smart, but for ease two team-bands can be crossed across the chest of ordinary school clothes, with a military paper hat, drums and drum sticks; paper epaulettes could be added for fun.

Pipers piping: Boat-shaped hats all the same colour with brightly coloured sashes across the chest, tin whistle.

Ladies dancing: Long pretty dresses, long gloves, cone-shaped hats with veil.

Lords a-leaping: Three-cornered hats with a feather, white ruffled shirts, bow-ties, long black trousers cut off at the knee and tightened with elastic, black plimsolls with silver foil buckles stuck on.

The Nativity

Traditional costumes for Mary and Joseph;
Shepherds: stripey material tied at the waist;
Angels: white shifts with tinsel in their hair;
Oxen, asses, sheep: masks can be made out of card
(see M. Grater, *Paper Faces* (Mills and Boon, 1967).

8   Rites of Passage

Rites of Passage

Theme

The next four assemblies are about the rites of passage, new beginnings at different times in the lives of different people. They include:

Baptism — a new life as a member of God's family for a baby or an adult; junior and senior soldiers — a new responsibility for a young person passing from childhood to adulthood as he/she promises to take responsibility for himself/herself and keep the faith;

a wedding — a new beginning for two people who make promises to each other;

Death — a new life.

5–11
Activity/Assembly

Baptism

Before the subject of baptism is discussed in assembly, it is most helpful if the theme of water has already been studied — the lovely feeling of being clean after a particularly dirty job, the life-giving drink of water to a thirsty man, the uses of water in our daily lives, etc. This can lead to a most natural thanksgiving service to God for his daily provision. Strong links can then be drawn between being made clean, receiving life, daily living and baptism.

Perhaps the class could visit a church and look at the font, or make a study of different fonts, or baptismal pools in the free churches. It is most helpful if a minister is invited into school to explain the meaning of baptism and the service itself. A display of Christening gowns could be set up. Perhaps some Christening presents could be displayed.

The most important aspect of baptism for the children to understand is that it is the outward sign of the beginning of a new life with God. The links then are clear: the symbolism of washing away sin; receiving the life-giving gift of the Holy Spirit; and daily living with Jesus.

It needs to be explained that when a baby is baptised, it is the parents or godparents who undertake the responsibility for the child to bring him up as member of the 'church' family and teach him all about faith in God. But, as we have already seen, this is only the beginning. Once the child can make decisions for himself and is willing to take responsibility for himself, then he must come to confirm his beliefs for himself at the special confirmation service. There also needs to be some explanation of adult baptism as practised by the Baptists and Pentecostalists. (see part 14 on pp. 256–8)

Prayer

We thank you Father, that we are all part of your world-wide family. Amen.

Hymn

No. 113, 'Family of Man' or No. 63, 'Sing Hosanna', in *New Life* (Galliard).

5–11
Assembly

Junior and Senior Soldiers

There is a turning point for young children in many faiths when children must profess their faith for themselves. The age at which this decision is taken varies from faith to faith, but usually takes place between 7 and 14 years. Roman Catholic children, for instance, make their first Holy Communion at about 7 or 8 years old; Salvation Army children do not have a communion service, but there is a special service for children to become 'Junior Soldiers'.

Generally, the children who will become Junior Soldiers will have attended primary church first. This is the class for 3–7-year-olds and teaches the children about the Bible through music, movement and mime. At 7 years of age the Salvation Army children are considered old enough to attend Junior meetings, where they learn more about the Bible and Salvation Army doctrines. When they are ready to make their promises to God for themselves, they are made Junior Soldiers at a special service at the Salvation Army citadel. They have to sign a card to show that their intentions are serious and that they promise to read their Bible and pray every day.

These Junior Soldiers then go on to an award scheme, where they have to work hard at various activities to obtain the bronze award. They have to pass eight activities in all to receive their badges. There are four compulsory sections such as reading the Bible, writing prayers, knowledge of the Army and being helpful; and there is another section from which children can choose four more activities e.g. learning a musical instrument, becoming proficient in art and craft, etc. Mothers and fathers have to sign the cards to say that their children have done these activities. Then the children can work towards their silver and gold awards.

Junior Soldiers sometimes join the singing group or the junior band which sings and plays instruments to people in old people's homes or hospitals. Junior Soldiers can only become Senior soldiers by attending special classes and doing a Bible correspondence course. Then at about 14 years of age there is a special swearing-in ceremony. The young people have to sign the 'Articles of War', which sets out all the beliefs held by Salvation Army members and which these children must profess in front of the full company, solemnly standing in front of their Army flag.

Either invite an Army officer into school for this assembly to explain the passage from Junior Soldier to Senior Soldier, or tell the children about it. Listen to some 'Army' music. Perhaps a 'helpful' scheme could be introduced into school, with teachers noting when children have been especially kind and helpful.

Prayer

Thank you, Father God, for all children everywhere, who commit themselves to your service and to helping others. Amen.

Hymn

No. 21, 'Hands to work and feet to run', in *Someone's Singing Lord* (A. and C. Black).

5–11
Assembly

A Wedding

Everybody loves a wedding, the beautiful clothes, the food and the presents, the excitement and preparation for the big day. A good starting point for this topic is to ask the children to bring in photographs of their parents' wedding, or grandparents' wedding, or to cut out pictures of weddings from newspapers or magazines.

Perhaps a real wedding dress could be borrowed and displayed, together with shoes, head-dress and veil, etc. A bridesmaid's dress and a page-boy's outfit could also be borrowed and displayed. This will provoke much good discussion, written work and art work. For handwriting practice, wedding invitations could be sent out from one class of children to all the other classes in the school. (Names can be copied from school registers.) Older children could draw up lists of wedding gifts, that they think are the essential items to have in the home. The cost of these items could be discussed. Younger children could draw the things they think they would need. Food for the wedding could be discussed, written about, or painted. Perhaps a model of a wedding cake could be made, or a caterer invited into school to tell the children about the kind of food he has prepared for a reception. Transport to and from the ceremony could be considered. How many ways could the couple travel to the reception? Paintings and models could support the answers — horse-drawn carriages, Rolls Royce cars, wheel-barrows, trains, etc. The ceremony itself should then be discussed. Where do couples get married? Try to find out about as many different places and types of service as possible.

Draw all the threads together by having a wedding assembly. Since the whole school has been invited, the children can all make special hats for the occasion, so that they can participate as guests. The class involved in the project (approximately thirty children) can take the following parts and will need appropriate costumes:

One bride
One groom
Four bridesmaids
Two page-boys
Two bride's parents
Two groom's parents
One minister
Fifteen choir members

These children could re-enact a simplified version of the wedding service either by reading the words on cards or by improvisation. A real treat for the whole school would be to let all the children share in the 'reception' afterwards by having a biscuit or piece of cake taken round by members of the 'wedding' class. It is amazing how a surprise piece of food in an assembly is regarded as a huge treat by all the children.

End with a simple prayer of thanks for all weddings everywhere.

Hymn

No. 15, 'Think of a world', from *Someone's Singing Lord* (A. and C. Black).

**7–11
Assembly**

Celebration of New Life After Death

Jesus said: 'I am the Resurrection and the Life. He who believes in me, though he die, yet shall he live.' (John 11: 25, *RSV*) Christians believe this wonderful promise that death is just the beginning of new life.

Let us look at the evidence of the risen Jesus. This could take the form of a series of brief playlets. Begin in the following way: Jesus is dead; his friends are terribly unhappy, confused and frightened.

> *First playlet*: The women go to the tomb and find the stone rolled away (Luke 24: 1–10).
>
> *Second playlet*: The two friends on the road to Emmaus (Luke 24: 13–32).
>
> *Third playlet*: The upper room; Thomas puts his hands on the nailed hands of Jesus (John 20: 24–29).
>
> *Fourth playlet*: Jesus eats breakfast on the beach with the fishermen (John 21: 1–14).

This subject needs very careful and sensitive handling with young children. Some children will already have experienced death of relatives or friends. Many others will not have any knowledge or understanding. (A very helpful book for 5-year-olds is *The Day Grandma Died*, adapted by J. Selby (Church Information Office).)

If the school is able to keep pets, then it becomes a natural part of the child's existence to experience death; this helps in coming to terms with this difficult subject. Grief should not be suppressed. The child should feel able to express his anger and grief. The positive hope of new life can bring great relief to a grief-stricken child; the four playlets are offered as one answer.

Hymn

No. 28, 'The journey of life', in *Someone's Singing Lord* (A. and C. Black) or No. 28, 'I danced in the morning', in *New Life* (Galliard); or No. 35 'He's back in the land of the living', in *New Life* (Galliard).

9   Water

5–11
Activity/Assembly

Water Projects

To begin this series of assemblies on water, set the scene by asking th
children to think about how water is used in their daily lives. Perhaps eac
class could focus on a particular aspect of water and be prepared to spea
about it when the classes join together for the first assembly.

For instance, one class could think about water in the home — cook
ing, washing, drinking, heating, etc.

Another class could think about water sports — swimming, wate
skiing, diving, fishing, canoeing, etc.

Another could think about water holidays — by the sea, on the rivers
canals, visits to ponds and lakes, etc.

Another could think about water in industry — canning, laundries
waterworks, power stations.

Others could think about the weather — rain, storms, clouds, etc.

Finally, one class could focus on the lack of water — what woul
this mean at home and abroad? (This could be developed in the secon
assembly.)

At this first assembly all the ideas need to be drawn together an
shared and discussed with the whole school. This can be done in a variet
of ways.

The children could be encouraged to make magazine picture collages
or paintings and drawings of a particular activity. Different shaped fis
mobiles could be cut out and suspended from the ceiling, or deep-sea tank
could be made out of old cardboard boxes.

When everyone has had a chance to contribute, show the Philip Gree
filmstrip on *Water*. (A very helpful book is Julian Cox, *The Water from you
Tap* (Wayland) 1982.)

Prayer

Heavenly Father, we thank you for your gift of water. We have learnt s
much about how we depend on water in our daily lives. Thank you
Amen.

Hymn

No. 7, 'Water of life', in *Come and Praise* (BBC).

5–11
Activity/Assembly

Lack of Water

For this assembly ask for one child volunteer to help you. Suggest the child runs on the spot until he/she is out of breath and thirsty. Then ask the children, 'What do they think this child needs? . . . Yes, a glass of water.' Give the child a drink, and then explain that many people in the world cannot have a drink of water when they most need it.

Perhaps the school could think about supporting the Oxfam scheme for buying a well or an irrigation pump in a country like India. If possible, invite an Indian mother to the assembly. Perhaps she could tell the children something about India. Posters from Oxfam could be displayed and sponsorship ideas could be discussed. Perhaps the children could make Indian almond sweets to sell in order to raise money.

Much good educational material is available from Oxfam on receipt of a stamped addressed envelope: Oxfam, 274 Banbury Road, Oxford OX2 7DZ (tel.: 086–556–777). Posters, wallcharts, worksheets and water pack are also available from: Christian Aid, PO Box No. 1, London SW9 8BH. The children's own awareness of the needs of others could be broadened through use of the material from these charitable organizations.

Prayer

Heavenly Father, We have so much in this country and we take our need for water for granted too easily. Help us to remember those who do not even have enough to drink, and help us to give generously of our time and efforts to support those schemes which provide basic water. Amen.

Hymn

No. 31, 'Because you care' or No. 32, 'The hungry man' in *Every Colour under the Sun* (Ward Lock Educational).

Clean and Dirty

Discuss the importance of being clean — for health, comfort and appearance. Ask the children to imagine what it would feel like to have jam on their fingers and to be unable to wash it off. Ask the children where clean water comes from and where it goes to. Talk about birds and animals needing to clean themselves.

Then tell the story about Jesus washing his friends' feet.

Remind the children about the supper that Jesus had in the upper room with his friends before he died. After the meal Jesus took a bowl of water and a towel, and he began to wash his friends' feet.

In those days the people wore open shoes and their feet used to get dusty and dirty.

The water was stored in large water pots. It was normally the custom for the servants of the household to wash the guests' feet.

Jesus loved his friends and wanted to show them that loving people will do anything for their friends.

Peter felt ashamed that he had not thought of washing Jesus' feet.

The disciples felt refreshed and clean and thanked Jesus for his loving care.

(For top juniors there is a beautiful sequence demonstrating this scene in the Scripture Union filmstrip/tape production of *The Champion*).

Prayer

Dear Lord Jesus, You gave us a lovely example of loving care for each other. Teach us to be more like you. Amen.

Hymn

No. 35, 'Take care of a friend' or No. 29, 'Such hard work', in *Every Colour under the Sun* (Ward Lock Educational).

5–7
Assembly

Moses

The whole class can be involved in this assembly, which is based on Exodus 1–2, through movement and music, dance and drama.
Divide the class into *groups*:

> soldiers
> mothers with babies
> reeds
> hand-maidens

and *main characters*:—

> King
> Captain of army
> Princess
> Mother
> Miriam
> Moses

Tell the story in the following way:

This is the story of how a baby was saved in a basket which floated on a river a long, long time ago.

The baby's name was Moses and he had a big sister called Miriam. They lived in the land of Egypt, where one day the King made a very cruel law. He said to his soldiers:

King: I am afraid that the Israelite people are becoming too powerful so I want you to kill all their baby boys. Throw them into the Nile.
Action: The army pretends to search the group of mothers, looking for their babies. [Then freeze.]
Moses' mother called her daughter Miriam and said: Quickly, let us make a basket out of the reeds from the river. If we cover the bottom with tar, it will be perfectly safe and watertight. Then we can hide our baby inside and float the basket on the river when the soldiers come to search our home.

Miriam did as she was told. She helped her mother to make the basket and place the baby inside. Then she ran to the river to hide the basket amongst the reeds.

Action: The reeds dance as Miriam hides the baby [tape-record some music for the reeds to dance to].

When Miriam was certain that the baby was quite safe in the reeds, she stood close by to make quite sure that nothing happened to him. Just then the King's own daughter came down to the water with all her beautiful maidens to have a swim.

Action: The princess and maidens perform a swimming dance [taped music is needed once more].

Suddenly, the princess saw the basket. She asked one of her servants to bring it to her. She opened the basket and saw the baby inside. He was crying. Miriam saw what had happened, and forgetting about being afraid, she ran up to the princess and said: 'Shall I go and find a nurse for you, who can look after the baby?' The princess replied: 'Yes, please.' So Miriam ran to fetch the baby's *own* mother. The princess said to her: 'If you look after this baby for me, I will pay you well.'

Later, when Moses was much older, he went to live in the royal palace with the princess. He grew up into a fine, strong man and he became a very great leader. This was all part of God's plan for him and the people of Israel. (See the second volume for the dramatic Pesah story).

Prayer

Father, we know that you had a wonderful plan for Moses. Help us to know your wonderful plan for each one of us. Amen.

Hymn

No. 17, 'Little baby Moses', in *Come and Sing* (Scripture Union).

5–7
Assembly

The Man Who Took Seven Baths

This Old Testament story from 2 Kings 5: 1–19 can be read from the Arch Book of the same title. (There are many other titles in this useful series.) A class of children can mime the actions. You will need the following characters:

Captain Naaman
100 captives
King
Several doctors
Naaman's wife
Wife's maid
Naaman's servants
Elisha
Elisha's servant

The story unfolds in the following way. Captain Naaman returns victoriously from war, bringing with him 100 captives. The King richly rewards Naaman by giving him twelve sacks of gold and twelve servants. Suddenly, they notice that Naaman has the dreaded skin disease (leprosy). Everyone runs away from him. Many doctors try to cure him, but all to no avail.

Naaman's wife has a little Israelite maid. The little maid tells her mistress that she knows a prophet in her own country who could cure Naaman. So Naaman sets out to see the King of this country, taking with him many chariots containing his servants and silver and gold to give to the King. The King sends Naaman to the Prophet Elisha. Elisha does not answer his door, but sends his servant out to tell Naaman that he must take seven baths in the River Jordan in order to be cured. Naaman flies into a rage, saying that he could have bathed in his own rivers and that he did not travel all this way just to bathe in the muddy River Jordan.

Naaman's servants plead with him to do what Elisha has commanded him to do. So Naaman decides to obey. He goes down to the Jordan and gets in and out of the water seven times. (Children can hold a large sheet to imitate the water movement.) Naaman's skin is healed. Naaman returns to Elisha's house once more and says: 'Now I know there is only one true God. Please accept these gifts.' But Elisha refuses and sends him home. End with a simple prayer of thanks for the little girl who saved her master.

Hymn

No. 10, 'Praise Him', in *Come and Sing* (Scripture Union).

5–6
Assembly

A Rain Dance

Read the story *Aio the Rain-maker* by Fiona French (Oxford University Press, 1975). This African folk tale lends itself to re-enactment in music and dance. The children could make African masks and make up their own rain dance to the beat of African drum music.

Prayer

Father, we know we can't make the rain fall, but we thank you for the joy of dance and the fun of making masks. Amen.

Hymn

No. 13, Second verse of 'We praise you for the sun', 'We praise you for the rain', in *Someone's Singing Lord* (A. and C. Black).

Calming Of The Storm

For those who live near the sea, try and arrange a visit to look at fishermen at work. Collect items for a display table — bits of driftwood, shells, cuttlefish, etc. Others will have to be content with a picture/book display about the sea.

Let the children mime the following story, with these characters:

Jesus
Six friends
Wind
Waves

Jesus had been talking to great crowds of people all day. He beckoned his friends and told them that he was tired. He asked his friends if they would sail him across the Sea of Galilee to the other shore where it was more peaceful. They agreed. All the friends got into a large boat and set sail. It was a calm evening. The fishermen knew the waters well. They had fished them for many years. Suddenly, the wind began to blow and buffet the little boat (a group of children perform the wind dance). Then the waves began to beat against the side of the boat. Jesus was so tired that he had fallen asleep. (The waves dance around the boat.)

At first the friends did not bother to wake Jesus; they just talked anxiously to each other. But then the waves became larger and stronger and rocked the boat and the friends became very frightened indeed. The friends woke Jesus up and said: 'We are in terrible trouble; the boat is sinking.' Jesus stood up and said, 'Peace, be still.' Immediately the wind ceased and the waves calmed, and Jesus said to his friends: 'Why were you so afraid? Don't you know that I will look after you?' But the friends looked at each other and said: 'Who is this man? Even the wind and waves obey him!'

Prayer

Dear Lord Jesus, You protected your friends in that storm on the Sea of Galilee. We ask you to protect all those who work at sea. Amen.

Hymn

No. 26, 'A little ship was on the sea', in *Child Songs*, ed. by Carey Bonner (The Pilgrim Press).

Water Poems For Movement

The following poems are from the excellent book edited by E.J.M. Woodland, *Poems for Movement* (Evans) reproduced by kind permission of Unwin
Hyman Ltd., which has been used by teachers for many years. They could
be read to the whole school to encourage participation in the assembly
theme by body movement.

The Rain

Pitter-patter, pitter-patter,
Little drops of rain,
Pitter-patter, pitter-patter
On the window pane.

Pitter-patter, pitter-patter,
Little drops of rain
Gently falling. Gently falling
To the ground again.

Pitter-patter, pitter-patter,
Little drops of rain
Running quickly. Running quickly,
Dance into a chain.

Here the children may imitate the rain-drops.

Verse 1: With head, arms and hands the children suggest the rain-drops
dashing against the window-pane and trickling down.
Verse 2: Arms and hands move gently downward. A whole body movement to the ground follows.
Verse 3: Here the children use the suggestion of running, then join hands
to suggest the rain-drops running together into trickles.

The Song of the Waves

We are the quiet, timid waves that gently
kiss your toe.

We hardly seem to move at all, so softly do
we flow.
The only sound we ever make is a whisper or
a sigh,
But inch by inch we creep along until the
tide is high.

We are the jolly, bubbling waves that laugh and
splash with glee.
We bustle up the seashore, as merry as can be.
We spill our foam upon the beach, spread like a
soapy pool,
Then slide back quickly to the sea and leave the
hot sand cool.

We are the heavy, roaring waves, that burst in
clouds of spray.
We crash against the cliff-side, and swirl and
spin away.
As each of us falls backwards, there's another
close behind
To hammer at the sturdy rock; to smash and tear
and grind.

Verse 1: Children make soft, flowing movements with hands, arms and
whole bodies, while gently moving forward.
Verse 2: Children use brisk, sharp movements of hands, arms and legs.
They move forward to suggest the waves breaking.
Verse 3: Here really strong, vigorous movements should be made with all
parts of the body.
(It helps to suggest that one end of the room represents the
beach.)

Prayer

Heavenly Father, We thank you for the soft refreshing rain that makes the
flowers grow and for all fun and joy of the seaside. Take care of each one
of us during the summer holidays. Amen.

Hymn

No. 9, 'To God who makes all lovely things', in *Someone's Singing Lord* A. and C. Black).

5–7
Activity/Assembly

Noah's Ark

Some religious education 'experts' have advised infant teachers not to tell the story of Noah's ark on the grounds that young minds cannot handle the story of a punishing God who floods the earth in order to wipe out evil. While I agree that I would not convey this message to 5-year-olds, I would nevertheless re-tell the story that Noah was a very good man, who was warned by God that there would be a flood and that he should build an ark and save his family and two of every kind of bird, insect and animal (Genesis chapters 6–9). To deny telling children this story is to deny them the chance to hear part of their cultural heritage. As children grow older the reason for the flood can be explained, but at the infant school level the story has rich opportunities for cross-curricular links and for young children to feel their way into the story through dance and drama, movement and mime and all kinds of art and craft and musical activities. To omit this story would be doing the children a disservice.

Reading/Writing/Language

1 Choose your favourite animal, describe its distinguishing features, write about what it eats, where it sleeps, approximate weight, shape and colour and finally why you like it best.
2 Write about 'creepy-crawlies' that you don't like. Draw pictures and make mobiles to hang from the ceiling of your classroom.
3 Make a class book about endangered species all over the world — panda, giant tortoise, etc.
4 Find out about the World Wildlife projects. Perhaps a speaker could be invited into school to show films, provide posters and share information: World Wildlife Fund, Panda House, 11–13 Ockford Road, Godalming, Surrey, GU7 1QU (Tel.: 04868 20551).
5 Visit a wildlife park, zoo or a bird sanctuary and find out all about the different species. Make a tape-recording of the different sounds. Be sure to keep a note of the animals recorded and approximate position on the tape. Make a class book about the expedition.
6 Find out about extinct animals, e.g. the dodo, the great auk.
7 Make a list of how animals sleep (see Masayuki Yabuuchi, *Sleep-*

ing Animals (Picture Corgi, 1987)), e.g. bats sleep upside down, flamingoes sleep on one leg.

8   Read Gerald Rose, *Trouble in the Ark* (Puffin Books/Kestrel, 1985) and make up your own list of sounds that animals make, e.g. moo, baa, hoot, squawk. These lists can be suspended from the ceiling in the classroom with pictures of the animals making that particular noise.

9   Make an ABC frieze to go right around the classroom with pictures/names of the animals under each letter.

10   Make individual topic books by researching different animals. — bears, gorillas, squirrels, etc. Books can be made in the shape of the animal. Older children can use reference books to help them. Younger children can write a single sentence on each page, e.g. 'Red squirrels have bushy tails.'

the tortoise is slow.

the cat is soft.

11 Play word games: make a collection of animal or bird sayings, e.g. as wise as an owl; make a collection of male and female animal names, e.g. fox and vixen; make a collection of mother and baby names, e.g. goose and gosling.

Mathematics

1 Make block graphs of your favourite animals/pets/colours.

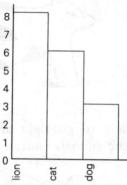

2 Learn the two times two multiplication table through the practical experience of handling two lots of two animals.
3 Weigh the class pet, and find out about weights of different animals. Record your results.
4 Find out about the different speeds of animals. Make a chart, divide it into three, draw fast animals on one side, slow animals on the other side and those in between in the middle.
5 Genesis 6: 14–16 tells us that the ark was approximately 133 metres long, 22 metres wide, 13 metres high. Give the children plenty of practical experience with metre sticks, click-wheels, etc. Perhaps the ark could be drawn by the older children in chalk on the playground — it would have to be a *very* large playground!
6 Make a model or drawing of the ark drawn to scale.

Science

1 *Floating and sinking*
Experiment with things that float and things that sink:
(i) Try different kinds of wooden off-cuts — oak, mahogany, balsa. Try to float all kinds of household items such as knives, forks, spoons, saucepans. Experiment with items around the classroom — paperclips, rubbers, pencils, straws.

(ii) Make a chart, divide the chart into two, write down all the things that float on one side, and all the things that sink on the other side.

(iii) Try to make a ball of plasticine (i.e. a sinker) float. Do this by hollowing out the centre and making the sides high until it floats.

2 *Water and air experiments*
Take two bottles of similar size, type and weight. Screw the tops on tightly, so that you have two bottles of air.

(i) Try floating the bottles on the water. What happens? (Bottles will float.)

(ii) Now reduce the amount of air in one bottle by adding some sand, float the bottles again. What happens? (The bottle with the sand will partly sink in the water.)

(iii) Repeat the experiment by adding more sand until the bottle sinks. (The explanation for this experiment is that the bottle containing sand weighs more than the bottle containing air, so the sand bottle sinks, while the air bottle floats.)

(iv) Make a study of different boats — yachts, oil-tankers, ships. Find out how a submarine can float and sink. (When a submarine submerges, water is let into the air tanks; for the submarine to float again, the water is pumped out and the tanks are filled with air.) See how this works by using a balloon and a deep water tray.

3 *Colour and light*
(i) How many colours are there in a rainbow? (Answer: red, orange, yellow, green, blue, indigo, violet.)

(ii) What are the primary colours of paint (red, yellow, blue); what are the primary colours of light (red, green, blue)? What will happen when you mix these colours using pieces of coloured perspex?

(iii) Try mixing red and blue paint together. What colour does it make? Mix red and yellow paint together. What do you find? Now try mixing yellow and blue paint. Record your experiments.

(iv) Make a coloured spinning top. You will need a circular piece of card. Paint the card with red, yellow, blue, green and orange paint. Put a pencil through the centre. Now spin the top. What happens to the colours? (They turn a whitish hue.) See also p. 180.

Art/Craft

There are many art/craft ideas that could be explored in connection with this theme.

1 Work large — make a huge frieze of the sea, sky, rainbow, ark with all the animals' heads poking out of the ark. Try to use different art techniques and fabrics to give a three-dimensional effect. For the background great fun can be had by all if the huge sheet of paper is first covered in swirling curling finger prints (use good finger paints). This could be overprinted when dry with luminous paints. All sorts of items such as cotton reels, potatoes, corks could be used to overpaint. To this could be added huge pieces of green, blue and white tissue paper or crêpe paper to make the waves of the sea. Painted fish can be suspended in the waves. The sky could be made of material collage, and the ark itself could be made out of strong cardboard projecting outwards from the flat paper by sticking matchboxes behind it (this gives the three-dimensional effect). Then every type of animal's face can peer out over the top of the ark. A huge rainbow can be made out of foil mosaics or tissue paper.

2 To give the classroom a 'watery' effect, different shaped fish and strips of green crêpe paper can be suspended from the ceiling (see fish shapes in M. Grater, in *One Piece of Paper* (Mills and Boon 1963).

3 Animal masks can be made for the animal dance assembly. These can either be very simple paper-bag masks or paper plates attached to dowling sticks and decorated by the children. (See C. Pitcher, *Masks and Puppets* (Franklin Watts, 1984) and B. Pflug *Funny Bags* (Worlds Work, 1970). Much more complicated masks can be made, but you would need to involve parents in the production (especially if the occasion was intended to be a full-scale end-of-term production). The best book for this type of mask is M. Grater, *Paper Faces* (Mills and Boon, 1967); the masks look very effective, but are quite difficult to make (even for adults!).

4 Junk models: all kinds of animals can be made for a classroom display, using cardboard boxes, toilet roll centres, egg boxes, yoghurt pots, etc. (See C. Pitcher, *Build Your Own Farmyard* (Franklin Watts, 1985).)

5 Make a large free-standing model of the ark, big enough for the children to play in. Huge cardboard boxes can be obtained from your local supermarket for this purpose. The ark doesn't have to be

elaborate, but could have a top that lifts off so that the children can climb inside and imagine what it feels like to be floating on the waves.

Music

There are some lovely hymns and songs associated with this theme, including the following:

No. 44, 'Who built the Ark', in *Someone's Singing Lord* (A. and C. Black, 1973).
No. 41, 'All things which live below the sky', in *Someone's Singing Lord* (A. and C. Black, 1973).
No. 38, 'The animals went in two by two', in *Apusskidu* (A. and C. Black, 1975).
No. 39, 'Going to the zoo', in *Apusskidu* (A. and C. Black, 1975).
No. 1, 'I have two ears', in *Count Me In* (A. and C. Black, 1984).
No. 37, 'Two in a boat', (Action Song) in *Count Me In* (A. and C. Black, 1984).
No. 44, 'Noah's birthday', in *Count Me In* (A. and C. Black, 1984).
No. 14, 'Act in song', in *Game-Songs with Prof. Dogg's Troupe* (A. and C. Black, 1983).
No. 18, 'Walking through the jungle', in *Game-Songs with Prof. Dogg's Troupe* (A. and C. Black, 1983).
No. 25, 'Colour song', in *Game-Songs with Prof. Dogg's Troupe* (A. and C. Black, 1983).
No. 38, 'Weather song', in *Game-Songs with Prof. Dogg's Troupe* (A. and C. Black, 1983).
No. 122, 'Butterflies are pretty things', in *Child Songs*, ed. by Carey Bonner (The Pilgrim Press reprint 1959).
No. 73, 'Down the air everywhere', in *Child Songs*, ed. by Carey Bonner (The Pilgrim Press).
No. 14, 'Who put the colours in the rainbow', in *Come and Praise* (BBC, 1978).

Assemblies

1   A book that re-tells the story of Noah's ark, using simple language and very imaginative, detailed pictures, is L.T. Lorimer, *Noah's*

Ark (Random Century House Pictureback, 1978). (There are also many others; see p. 167.) Reading the story and pouring over the pictures is a very good way to introduce the subject, expecially if it is intended that the story will be used as a drama production for an assembly.

Every child could be involved in a class assembly; and it is even possible to involve the whole school in the drama by sitting in-the-round, wearing simple masks and getting children to march or dance round the centre when their particular section is called: e.g. all the insects parade round, pretending to board the ark; all the 'cats' show us how they eat; all the birds fly around before roosting. Children can dance to music from *Carnival of the Animals* by Saint Saëns, or many other classical pieces of music can be used.

2 A simpler variation on the above theme is to read John Ryan's *Mr Noah's Birthday* (Beaver Books, 1981). (There are many more Noah story books in this series; see list below.) The story is so well told that it can be read aloud to the whole school while the class mime the various parts: e.g. Mrs Noah gives Mr Noah a mug; Shem, Ham and Japheth give their presents; the animals tune up ready for a concert. The music for the concert gets lost, but the story ends happily, with all the animals singing their 'sound' to the music of 'Old Macdonald Had a Farm', only with the words, 'Mr Noah had an ark'. Many more songs could be added to complete the assembly (see list in music section above).

3 Other related themes for assemblies could take the form of art work and writing about endangered species: the work of the World Wildlife Organisation, descriptions of visits to zoos, bird sanctuaries and wildlife parks; care of pets; protection of birds and bird nests; insects and mini-beasts. The children could be encouraged to write their own simple prayers to accompany the work.

4 Visitors from various animal sanctuaries or charities could be invited to school to talk to children about their work, e.g. PDSA, RSPCA, RSPB. Perhaps children could make a special collection for a particular charity.

5 In some parts of the country specialists will come into school and bring their animals, birds or insects for the children to see, e.g. a police horse, or owls that have grown up in captivity, or a beekeeper might describe his work.

6 A 'Thank you God assembly' for the creepy-crawlies that nobody likes could be presented in words and dancing to the song 'The Ugly Bug Ball'.

Stories

Noah's Ark Stories

The following are written by John Ryan 1980/81 and published by Hamyn: *Roll Call on The Ark, All Aboard! Crockle Saves the Ark, The Weather Forecast, Crockle Takes a Swim, The Haunted Ark, Mr Noah's Birthday, Crockle Flies a Kite, Crockle Adrift, The Floating Jungle, Action Stations!* and *The Frozen Ark.*

Other Noah Books

BAXTER, L. *Noah and the Ark* (Macdonald, 1983).
HUTTON, W. *Noah and the Great Flood* (Hamish Hamilton, 1977).
STORR, C. *Noah and His Ark* (Franklin Watts, 1982) (top Infants could read this version for themselves).
Starter Legends: Noah and the Flood (Macdonald, 1973).

Story Books with Animals/Creatures as Main Characters

BURNINGHAM, J. *Mr Gumpy's Outing* (Jonathan Cape, 1970). Picture Puffin 1986.
CARLE, E. *The Bad-Tempered Ladybird* (Puffin, 1982)
CARLE, E. *The Very Hungry Caterpillar* (Hamish Hamilton, 1970). Picture Puffin 1987.
GRETZ, S. *The Bears Who Went to the Seaside* (Puffin, 1975). Black 1958.
HUTCHINS, P. *Rosie's Walk* (Bodley Head 1968). Picture Puffin, 1983, English and Urdu.
KERR, J. *Mog the Forgetful Cat* (Collins, 1983).
KRASILOVSKY, P. *The Cow Who Fell in the Canal* (Picture Puffins Reprint, 1974).
McKEE, D. *Elmer, The story of the Patchwork Elephant,* (Anderson Press, Revised Edition, 1989).
PIERS, H. *The Mouse Book* (Methuen, 1966).
ZION, G. *Harry the Dirty Dog* (Bodley Head, 1960.) Picture Puffin 1970.

Poetry

There are many useful poetry books with an emphasis on animals or counting animals. Here are just a few:

BROOK, J. *Mrs. Noah's ABC 123* (World's Work, 1979).
EDWARDS, D. *Listen and Play Rhymes Book One* (Methuen, 1973).
GIBSON, J. and WILSON, R. *Red and Black Rhyme Book* (Macmillan, 1967).
HALEY, G. *One Two Buckle My Shoe* (World's Work, 1965) (a book of counting rhymes).
MATTERSON, E, *This Little Puffin* (Puffin, 1969) (this is also an excellent anthology).
MILLIGAN, SPIKE. *Silly Verse for Kids* (Penguin, 1959, Puffin 1970.)
SAMSON, C. *Counting Rhymes* (A. and C. Black, 1974).
SAMSON, C. *Speech Rhymes* (A. and C. Black, 1974).
SAMSON, R. *Rhythm Rhymes* (A. and C. Black, 1964).
WOODLAND E.J.M. (Ed.) *Poems for Movement* (Evans, 1966).

Environmental Studies

Start with the children's own environment.

1 *Observe small animals*: snails, slugs; look at how they move; what they eat, etc. Examine under a microscope. Be sure to return the animal to its natural habitat.
2 *Minibeast project*: all kinds of insects can be observed. Make careful observational drawings. Research habitats, food, etc. Discuss life-cycles, e.g. caterpillar to butterfly.
3 *Set up a bird table*. Encourage the children to feed the birds and make careful recordings of the birds that visit the bird table. Make sure the children know that they must never take birds' eggs. However, a discarded nest could be observed carefully, and materials used to make the nest could be identified and noted. Discuss migration: which birds migrate (see p. 179)?
4 *Make a study of class pets*: how to look after the pet; what they eat, where they sleep; cleanliness, etc.
5 *Farm animals*: perhaps a visit to a farm could be arranged. Make a study of large and small animal farming.
6 *Wild animals*
   (i) First make a study of wild animals in this country, e.g. fox, badger.
   (ii) Then animals overseas could be researched, e.g. elephants, rhinos.
   (iii) Endangered species could be studied, e.g. panda (see Resources below).

(iv)   *Wild animals in captivity*: make a study of this topic. When is it necessary to keep wild animals in captivity?
7   *Camouflage*: which insects or animals use camouflage to protect themselves? (Examples are moths, tigers, chameleons.)
8   Sea creatures
  (i)   Make a study of sea mammals, e.g. whales, dolphins.
  (ii)   Make a study of fish. Discuss the difference between mammals and fish. (Mammals are warm-blooded and breathe air; fish are cold-blooded and breathe through gills in water.)

Resources

Environmental Studies

The MacDonald Starters cover a wide range of topics including frogs, snakes, bees, beetles, spiders, butterflies, ants, bears, whales, farms. In addition the following books are useful:

BENSON, B. *The Hare* (Cambridge University Press, 1977).
BENSON, B. *The Polar Bear* (Cambridge University Press, 1978). (a Pole Star Book; there are many more books in this series).
HOFFMAN, M. *Bear* (Windward/Belitta Press, 1986).
HOFFMAN, M. *Tiger* (Windward/Belitta Press, 1983).
LANE, M. *The Squirrel* (Methuen Childrens Books, 1981).
LEIGH-PEMBERTON, J. *Bears and Pandas* (Ladybird Books, 1979) (there are many excellent reference books in the Ladybird series).
PLUCKROSE, H. *Whales* (Hamish Hamilton, 1979).
SIMON, N. and XUQI, J. *The Giant Panda* (J.M. Dent and Sons, 1986).
SINGER A. *Wild Animals from Alligator to Zebra* (Random House, 1973).
SNOW, K. *I Am a Badger* (World's Work, 1979).
THOMPSON, B. (Ed.) *Monkeys, Gorillas and Chimpanzees* (Sidgwick and Jackson, 1974).
FIRST INTEREST BOOKS published by Ginn 1966/67 contain the following titles: *Save These Animals, Animals Keeping Clean, Animal Defences, Dolphins and Whales, Birds' Feet and Beaks.*
The Zoo books published by GINN are an excellent reference series. Real photographs are used and important facts are conveyed in e.g. *The African Elephant.*
The Read about It series includes the following by O.B. Gregory: *The Big Cats,* Book 114, *Wild Cattle,* Book 120, *Rhinos and Zebras,* Book 117, *Kangaroos and Other Marsupials,* Book 112. There are approximately 120 books in this excellent series published by Wheaton.

Science

BRANLEY, F.M. *Floating and Sinking* (A. and C. Black, 1968).
JAMES, A. *Floating Things*, Starters Science (Macdonald Educational, 1973).
SHOWELL, R. *Let's Look at Colour* (Galt Educational, 1985).
SHOWELL, R. *Sounds all Round* (Galt Educational, 1985).
WARD, A. *Flight and Floating* (Usborne Publishing, 1981).

Art/Craft

CAKET, C. *Infant Crafts: Things to Make at Home and School* (Blandford Press, 1983).
CURTIS A. and HINDLEY, J. *The Know How Book of Paper Fun* (Usborne Publishing, 1975).
GERLINGS, C. and IVES, S. *Noah's Ark in Paper and Card* (B.T. Batsford, 1974).
GRATER, M. *Fun Figures* (Macdonald, 1987).
GRATER, M. *One Piece of Paper* (Mills and Boon, 1963).
GRATER, M. *Paper Faces* (Mills and Boon, 1967).
HART, T. *Art and Craft* (Kaye and Ward, 1984).
HUTCHINGS, M. *Making Old Testament Toys* (Mills and Boon, 1972).
LOISELOT, C. NICOSTRATE *The Papier Mâché Book* (Methuen Children's Books, 1986).
MACDONALD *Colourcrafts Animals I* (Macdonald, 1971, 1984).
MACDONALD *Colourcrafts Animals II* (Macdonald, 1971, 1984).
PFLUG, B. *Funny Bags* (World's Work, 1970).
PINDER, P. *Simple Printmaking* (Search Press, 1977).
PITCHER, C. *Build your own Farmyard* (Franklin Watts, 1985).
PITCHER, C. *Masks and Puppets* (Franklin Watts, 1984).
PLUCKROSE, H. *Collage Ideas* (Evans Brothers, 1979).
TENKO, F. and SIMON, E. *Paperfolding to Begin With* (World's Work, 1969).
VAUGHAN, J. (Ed.) *Prints and Patterns*, Starter Activities (Macdonald Educational, 1973).

Assemblies

CAMPBELL, E. *Sometimes When I Get Scared* (Pickering and Inglis, 1981).
DAVIDSON, S. *Infant Assemblies* (Scripture Union, 1983).
FARNCOME, A. *It's Our Assembly* (NCEC, 1979).
FARNCOME, A. *Let's Plan an Assembly* (NCEC, 1985).
FISHER, R. *Together with Infants* (Evans Brothers, 1982).

PURTON R. and STOREY, C. *First Assemblies* (Basil Blackwell, 1981).
SMITH, K.N. *Themes in Religious Education* (Macmillan, 1969).
VAUSE, D. *The Infant Assembly Book* (Macdonald, 1985.)

Counting Books

CARLE, E. *1, 2, 3 to the Zoo* (Hamish Hamilton, 1969).
LYSTER, M. *Counting Zoo Animals* (Blackie, 1979) (photographs).
MOSLEY, F. *Animal Numbers* (Patrick Hardy, Books 1984).
TAFURI, N. *Who's Counting* (J. MacRae Books, 1986).
YOUNGS, B. *One Panda* (Bodley Head, 1980).

Filmstrips

Philip Green Educational Limited, 112a Alcester Road, Studley, Warwickshire B80 7NR (tel.: 0527 854711) has produced some lovely filmstrips which could be used in conjunction with this topic: *Birds, Wings and Things, Bees, Pets, Zoo Animals, Small Creatures.*

5
Assembly

A 'Thank You' Book About Water

For this final assembly make a large booklet in the shape of a drop of water:

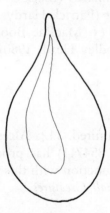

Ask each child to draw a special 'thank you' picture which can be pasted inside. A little preparation is needed to prevent duplication. Read it together during the final assembly. As each page is turned, the children could say, 'Thank you, God.'

Hymn

No. 14, 'Stand up, clap hands, shout thank you, Lord', in *Someone's Singing Lord*, (A. and C. Black).

10   Animals and Birds

5–7
Activity/Assembly

Farm Animals — Sheep Farming

Show the children a shepherd's crook and ask if anyone knows what it is. Then ask them whether the crook shown is a neck or a leg crook. Do they know the difference? (Neck crooks are much wider than leg crooks.)

Perhaps some sheep's wool can be taken into school to show the children. Different groups could try dyeing it different colours using vegetable dyes.

Explain the work of a sheep farmer. Stress that it is very hard work farmers have to get up very early and in all weathers to feed the sheep, to count them and check them over (called 'lookering') and to make sure that none of them has gone astray.

Remind the children of the sheep farming year: lambing in the spring, sometimes bottle-feeding lambs who have lost their mothers (called 'sock lambs'); shearing in the summer; dipping to prevent disease in the summer and autumn; clipping and cleaning feet and bottoms against foot-rot and disease; changing the sheep from one field to another to give them new pasture and fresh grass; rounding up the sheep to inject against various ailments and drench against worms and liver fluke; going to market to sell young lambs and the wool in the autumn; making hay for the sheep to eat during the winter snows; selecting the ewes to make up the new flock for the next year, etc.

Ask a group of children to paint these various activities before the assembly. These can be mounted and displayed and discussed before telling the story 'A Lamb Called "Nuisance".'

A Lamb Called 'Nuisance'

Mrs Brown was ill in bed. Farmer Brown had to go out all day to buy new machinery. But it was lambing time and although most of the ewes had lambed successfully, Farmer Brown was extremely worried about one ewe who had had twins early that morning. Although the ewe was feeding the first lamb quite happily, she was neglecting the other lamb because it looked so sick and weakly. Farmer Brown knew that unless the lamb fed from its mother very quickly, the mother would reject the lamb completely and it would die.

'I'm terribly worried about that ewe and her two lambs — she doesn't seem to be feeding the second lamb at all. I know you are not well, my dear', Mr Brown said to Mrs Brown, 'but could you just look out of the window during the morning and see if the second lamb is all right.' 'Oh dear', said Mrs Brown, 'I don't feel at all well, but I will keep an eye on the lamb.'

Mr Brown set off and Mrs Brown went back to bed. At about coffee time Mrs Brown looked out the window. She stood watching silently for a minute or two and then to her horror she saw the ewe that Mr Brown had mentioned pushing a very sickly lamb away from her. The ewe butted the lamb so hard that the lamb fell over and then the ewe marched off with her healthy lamb. Mrs Brown could hear sad little cries of 'baa, baa' coming from the sickly lamb, but then she saw it get up and follow its mother.

'Oh dear', thought Mrs Brown, 'if I go and get the lamb now, I might frighten the mother ewe altogether and she may never take it. I had better leave the lamb to follow its mother.'

Sometime later Mrs Brown looked out the window again. This time the mother ewe was far more ferocious and butted the lamb into the air. But the brave little lamb got up and followed its mother once more. Mrs Brown didn't know what to do. On the one hand, she could see that the mother wasn't taking to her lamb, but on the other hand, the lamb seemed determined to stay with its mother. So once more Mrs Brown decided not to interfere.

It was about tea-time when Mrs Brown looked out the window again; this time Mrs Brown could see the mother ewe and her healthy lamb, but she couldn't see the sickly lamb anywhere. 'Oh dear, what a nuisance,' thought Mrs Brown, 'I feel so ill, but I will just have to put on my dressing-gown and walk down the field and search for that baby lamb.'

It was a very long way to the bottom of the field and poor Mrs Brown, dressed in her dressing-gown and wellies, tramped over the long wet grass looking everywhere for the lost lamb. 'Where are you?' she called, 'Oh, where are you?' Suddenly, she heard a weak little bleat coming from the patch of grass just ahead of her. She hurried forward and there in the long grass lay the tiny white lamb. It was so exhausted from trying to catch up with its mother, and it was so weak from having no food that Mrs Brown thought that it was dying. The lamb did not move. Mrs Brown bent down and carefully put the lamb inside her dressing-gown. The lamb was so cold and shivery, that Mrs Brown was certain the lamb would not live.

'Oh,' she whispered, 'you are such a nuisance. I don't feel well myself, and I certainly don't feel like carrying you all the way back to the house. But I will. Come along, here we go.' Mrs Brown trudged back up the field to the house, the lamb felt heavier with every step and Mrs Brown felt more and more tired. When she got indoors, Mrs Brown put the lamb in a box by the kitchen cooker. But the lamb did not move, its head rolled forward and it was too weak even to bleat.

Mrs Brown could not find the baby milk and bottle that was always kept in the farmhouse, so she just did not know what to do to save the lamb. Suddenly, she thought, 'I will phone Mr Brown at the machinery sale, he will know how to save the lamb.' So Mrs Brown dialled the number. 'I am afraid that we ran out of the baby milk yesterday. Can you make up some warm sugar-water and dip a piece of cloth into it for the lamb to suck?' Mr Brown said, 'I hope that will keep the baby lamb alive until I can get home and bring the special milk and the baby bottle.'

Mrs Brown quickly made up the warm water and dipped a clean piece of sheet into it. But the lamb was too weak to suck. So Mrs Brown dipped her finger into the water and the lamb started to suck very gently. But it was a very slow process, and the kitchen floor was cold and hard and Mrs Brown was feeling very ill. 'You are a nuisance,' she whispered, 'but you have just got to drink.' Mrs Brown sat with the lamb for two hours, giving it drips of the sugar-water on her finger and then on the piece of rag. Miraculously, the lamb held on until Mr Brown came home with the milk and the baby bottle. Mr Brown made up the warm powdery milk and after trying very hard, the little lamb started to suck. However, she still looked very weak and sickly, and Mr Brown was afraid that she would not live through the night. They made her warm and comfortable for the night and then they went to bed. Mr and Mrs Brown took it in turns to try and feed the lamb every two hours during the night.

In the morning the little lamb was sitting up and bleating. Farmer Brown quickly made up some more milk and to his astonishment, the little lamb sucked very hard and drank half the bottle. Mr and Mrs Brown again took it in turns to feed the lamb throughout that day and the next night and the next day and night, until on the third day the little lamb struggled to get out of her box and began to follow Mrs Brown round the kitchen.

'She doesn't know she's a lamb, she thinks she's our baby', laughed Mrs Brown. And that's when she got her name 'Nuisance'. While it was funny at first to be followed everywhere, it soon became very tiresome, especially when the lamb went to the toilet on the Brown's best sitting-room carpet, and even followed Mr Brown into the shower and then proceeded to put wet hoof marks all the way down the stair-carpet. 'Oh, you are a nuisance', the Browns both said. 'She will have to join the rest of the flock', said Mr Brown two weeks later. She's really becoming a nuisance in the house.

Nuisance didn't want to join the rest of the flock and stayed close to Mr and Mrs Brown, but quite suddenly when she saw all the other lambs chasing round the field and skipping and gambolling, she set off without a backward glance, and ran off to play with them.

It was a very strange thing, that Nuisance really knew her name and whenever Mr and Mrs Brown called 'Nuisance', 'Nuisance', she would come running up to them, wherever they were in the field.

But the story doesn't end there. Two or three years later, when Nuisance was a mother ewe herself, Farmer Brown himself was ill, and Mrs Brown had to move the whole flock to a new pasture on her own. It's quite difficult to move sheep on one's own, as any farmer will tell you, because unless you are very careful, they will go off in all different directions. But Mrs Brown shouted, 'Nuisance, come on Nuisance, you have got to lead the way to the new field. If you come, all the others will follow you.' And do you know, that's exactly what they did.

If you know any farmers, perhaps you could feed a sock lamb in school and bring it into the assembly.

Prayer

Heavenly father, We thank you for all farmers and for the work they do. Be with them in times of difficulty and hardship. Give them the strength to work very long hours, for our benefit. Amen.

Hymn

No. 14 'Stand up, clap hands, shout thank you Lord', in *Someone's Singing Lord* (A. and C. Black).

5–7
Assembly

A Sleepy Dance for Hibernating Animals

Some music that embodies changes of mood from quick action to slow movement; some simple props, i.e. a cardboard 'shell' for the tortoise; some spikes for the hedgehog; simple masks for:

Frogs) These all
Newts) hibernate,
Grass snake) although the hedgehog
Tortoise) has been known to wake up
Hedgehog) on a mild winter night.
Dormouse) His sleep is *not* continuous. He wakes up, has a good meal and then goes back to sleep.
Squirrel) Strictly speaking, the squirrel does not hibernate, but takes long naps and then wakes up during the winter and hunts for his store of food.

A very useful book for help with making masks is Grater, *Complete Book of Paper Mask Making*, Dover Books, 1984.

Read the detailed descriptions of how and where each of the above animals hibernates in 'The Observer's Book of Wild Animals', published by Frederick Warne and then let the children choose which animal they would like to be in the hibernation dance.

For instance, groups of children portraying the frogs and wearing frog masks can begin with large leaps across the hall, until they come to rest 'embedded in mud at the pond-bottom, or in damp holes in the earth'. Then the green grass snakes could do a slithering dance before coming to rest and curling up under the roots of a tree to pass the winter in sleep.

Take each of the animals in turn, so that the whole class can participate in the hibernation dance. End with a simple prayer of thanks to God for his provision for the animals in winter.

Hymn

No. 54, 'Look for signs that summer's done', in *Someone's Singing Lord* (A. and C. Black).

Miracle of Migration

Perhaps the children could set up a bird table to feed the birds that winter in Britain. Make a chart that can be divided into two. On one side list all the birds that migrate; on the other side list all the birds that remain in Britain.

Keep a nature diary and note the date or dates when large groups of swallows gather together to make their great flight to their winter home in Africa. Watch the birds perch on telephone wires before they set off on their journey of hundreds of miles. If the children keep a bird diary throughout the winter, they could watch for the first signs of spring by watching to see when the swallows return. Not only do the birds find their way across continents without signposts or anyone telling them the way, but they often return to the very same spot in the very same garden that they left at the end of the summer.

A group of children could tell the school about the birds that migrate and those birds that remain in Britain and about their observations at the bird table.

The school could be encouraged to make a collection for the Royal Society for the Protection of Birds, The Lodge, Sandy, Bedfordshire SG19 2DL (tel.: 0767 80551).

Prayer

Heavenly Father, We thank you for the miracle of migration. We know that you care for even the tiniest sparrow. Bless the birds on their journey to warmer climates and help us to remember to care for the birds that remain here. Amen.

Hymn

No. 43, 'Little birds in winter time', in *Someone's Singing Lord* (A. and C. Black) or No. 24, 'A little tiny bird', in *Someone's Singing Lord* (A. and C. Black).

5–7
Assembly

Pets

Prepare a pet-graph prior to this assembly with numbers up the side of the chart, pets along the bottom, some coloured sticky paper, cut into squares, to stick on the chart to illustrate graphically each pet owned by the children.

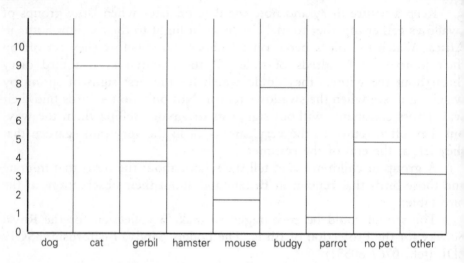

Ask the children who has a pet? Allow different children to come up to the chart and stick on a piece of sticky paper to represent their pet. (This chart could be passed around the classrooms later in the day so that all the children can have a chance to say what sort of pet they have at home.)

Prepare one class beforehand to paint their pet and stand up in the hall and tell the rest of the children about their pet. Some children may not have pets, because they live in a high rise flat or on busy roads. If the school has pets, perhaps the children without pets of their own could paint the school pet, or the pet they would like to have.

Prepare another group of children to talk about caring for their pets. What do they need? Encourage the children to talk about feeding, cleaning, warmth, loving, grooming, walking, keeping them out of harm's way on bonfire night, etc. Emphasize this point by taking a caged bird into school.

I was fortunate enough to obtain an opera-singing parrot, who could also laugh hysterically. When the children were singing the first hymn, the parrot joined in (to the joy and amusement of the whole school), and when the children started laughing, the parrot out-laughed them all. It served as in important reminder to the children that pets can bring us much joy and laughter, but they cannot go shopping and buy their own food; they cannot clean their own cages; they need love and companionship and, most of all, they need to be taken care of. Children need to be warned about never being cruel to animals, and that if they look after their pets, they will be rewarded by great joy and happiness.

Prayer

Heavenly Father, We thank you for all the joy and happiness that pets can bring. May we never hurt or harm our pets. Help us to remember to be kind and to clean and feed our pets every day. Bless those who look after pets that have been ill-treated. Amen.

Hymn

No. 42, 'I love God's tiny creatures', in *Someone's Singing Lord* (A. and C. Black).

5–11
Assembly

The Lost Sheep

(Adapted from an idea in Judy Gattis Smith, *Show Me*, Creative Resources Two, (Bible Society, 1985).)

Make a happy and a sad mask out of brown paper bags. Tell the story of the lost sheep using the *Good News Bible*, Luke 15: 1–7.

Help the children to explore the feelings of the shepherd; first his *anguish* over one missing lamb after he has counted ninety-nine and re-counted them to make quite sure that one is missing; then his *fear* that a wolf might have taken the lamb; then his *concern*, looking in all the likely places that the lamb might be trapped; finally, his *joy* when he hears a weak little bleat and his feelings of great *happiness*, when he finds the lamb unharmed, but stuck in a rocky crevice.

Recount how he rushes home to tell all his friends that he has found the lost lamb and how he decides to invite his friends to a special celebratory party.

Then it's the children's turn. One child puts on the unhappy mask and retells the story in his own words, trying to describe the shepherd's unhappy feelings. Another child puts on the happy mask and plays the part of the joyful shepherd. Variations on this theme include characters from the Bible portraying fear and bravery, nice or nasty.

The book *Show Me* is well worth buying. It is intended for 3–13-year-olds, and it is packed with many useful ideas and activities for drama in RE and school assemblies.

Prayer

Dear Lord Jesus, We know that you are like the good shepherd who cares for each one of us. Protect us from any danger today and look after those we love and those who love us. Amen.

Hymn

No. 28, 'Loving shepherd of thy sheep', in *Infant Praise* (Oxford University Press).

THE GOOD SHEPHERD

Psalm 23: 1–6, *Good News Bible*
　　Teach one of the psalms, i.e. Psalm 23 or Psalm 150 as a choral speaking piece. It can be a very dramatic way of ending 'The Lost Sheep' assembly, if it is done well, paying attention to loud and soft phrasing.

Psalm 23

The Lord is my shepherd;
I have everything I need.
He lets me rest in fields of green grass
and leads me to quiet pools of fresh water.
He gives me new strength.
He guides me in the right paths
as he has promised.
Even if I go through the deepest darkness,
I will not be afraid, Lord,
for you are with me.
Your shepherd's rod and staff protect me.

5–9
Assembly

Pin the Load on the Donkey

Begin by reading Matthew 11: 28, *Good News Bible*: 'Come to me all of you who are tired from carrying heavy loads and I will give you rest.' (Quotation from the *Good News Bible*, published by Bible Society/Collins is reproduced with the permission of the publishers).

For this activity you will need:

a large outline of a donkey (with no tail)
a tail
a blindfold
an easel or stand on which to pin the outline of the donkey
a bag that can be pinned onto the donkey's back
several word cards with words such as: 'selfish', 'greedy', 'spiteful', 'unkind', 'lazy' and some blank cards and a pen for extra words.

Ask the children if they have ever played 'Pin the tail on the donkey'. Then ask for a volunteer to be blindfolded to try to pin on the donkey's tail. Let several children try. After the fun and laughter, explain the serious message that people take a great deal of trouble about how they look on the outside (i.e. smart looking donkey with his tail), but sometimes they are not very nice inside.

Further explain that the donkey is used to carrying heavy weights, so pin the bag on his back and inform the children that you are going to fill up the bag with all the heavy weights that people carry about with them. Explain that a 'heavy weight' can be anything nasty that we think or do that spoils us and makes us feel unhappy. When we have got rid of all these heavy loads, we will all feel a lot lighter, brighter and happier, and look nicer on the outside too.

Using the prepared cards, read out the words clearly to the whole school: 'selfish', 'greedy', 'spiteful', 'unkind', 'lazy'.

Then choose a word, e.g. 'selfish'. Tell the children why you have selected this word (or insert others of your own), and then describe an incident illustrating how you have been selfish this week. Put the word into the donkey's bag. Encourage the children to reflect on the prepared words, e.g. 'lazy' — this is, not picking up rubbish, or not picking up their coats off the floor, and ask for volunteers to pin these words into the baskets on the donkey's back. Then ask the children if there are any other things weighing them down. (Use the spare cards and explain that any-thing that makes us unhappy inside can be written down and added to the donkey's load.) Finally, tell the children that Jesus said: 'Come to me, all of you who are tired from carrying heavy loads, and I will give you rest.' Ask the children to try and imagine Jesus sitting on the donkey carrying all our heavy loads so that we can look just as nice inside as we do on the outside.

Prayer

Dear Lord Jesus, We ask you to help us to be kind instead of unkind; generous instead of greedy; loving instead of spiteful; unselfish instead of selfish; hardworking instead of lazy. For your name's sake. Amen.

Hymn

No. 38, 'Think, think on these things', in *Someone's Singing Lord* (A. and C. Black).

11   Our Senses

7–11
Activity/Assembly

<h2 style="text-align:center">Sight</h2>

The aim of this assembly is to help children to become aware of the miracle of sight. By looking at each other's eyes, noticing the colour and shape, learning about the parts of the eye, discussing what can be seen, from the tiniest flower to a beautiful sunset, the children will be helped to achieve this aim.

In realizing how fortunate sighted people are, children need to become aware of what it might be like to be blind, and move beyond the classroom to consider ways in which sighted people can help blind people. There are various ideas below to encourage this involvement.

By engaging in some of the fun ideas suggested, such as trying optical illusions, considering the wonder of animals' eyes and the magnificent eyes of a bird of prey, by really looking and observing with a magnifying glass, it is hoped that children will be led to give thanks to God for this gift of sight.

Discussion Points

1   Discuss the miracle of sight. What can you see in the classroom, outside, in the street, in the garden, in the sky?

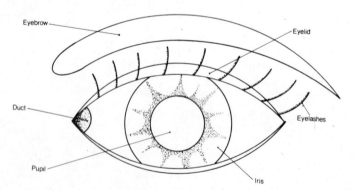

2   Discuss animal's eyes. Which animals have eyes in the front and which have eyes at the side, and why? Which creature can move each eye separately (e.g. chameleon). What would it be like for humans?

3   Discuss colours, favourite colours, mixing colours, etc.
4   Discuss the power of light.
5   What can you see with a telescope, binoculars, periscope, magnifying glass?
6   Discuss optical illusions (see Figures 7 and 8).
7   Finally, discuss what it must be like to be blind.

Follow-up Activities for the Children

Written Work

1   Make a graph of the different eye colours of the members of your class (see Figure 9).
2   Write about what you think it would be like to be blind.
3   Read the poem by Norman MacCaig, 'An Ordinary Day' in R. Deadman and A. Razzell, *Awareness 1* (Macmillan, 1977) Perhaps you could write your own poem.
4   Make a pair of green cellophane spectacles. Write about what your world looks like when wearing them.

An Ordinary Day

I took my mind for a walk
Or my mind took me for a walk —
Whichever was the truth of it.

The light glittered on the water
Or the water glittered in the light.
Cormorants stood on a tidal rock

With their wings spread out,
Stopping no traffic. Various ducks
Shilly-shallied here and there

On the shilly-shallying water.
An occasional gull yelped. Small flowers
Were doing their level best

To bring to their kerb bees like
Aerial charabancs. Long weeds in the clear
Water did Eastern dances, unregarded

By shoals of darning needles. A cow
Started a moo but thought
Better of it ... And my feet took me home

And my mind observed to me,
Or I to it, how ordinary
Extraordinary things are or

How extraordinary ordinary
Things are, like the nature of the mind
And the process of observing.

Reproduced by kind permission of Norman MacCaig.

(*Source*: R. Deadman and A. Razzell, *Awareness I*, Macmillan, 1977.)

Religious and Moral Education

1   Many books tell the story of Louis Braille. An excellent example is S. Keeler, *Louis Braille* (Wayland, 1986).
2   Write to the Royal National Institute for the Blind, at 224 Great Portland Street, London WIN 6AA, asking for a card copy of the Braille alphabet (enclose a s.a.e.) (see Figure 6).
3   Perhaps you could start a silver paper collection to buy a guide dog for a blind person. You could do this by writing to: Guide Dogs for the Blind Association, Director of Appeals, 9–11 Park Street, Windsor, Berks SL4 1JR (tel.: 0753 855711).
4   There is much biblical material such as (i) Jesus restoring sight to the blind man (Mark 10: 46–52), (ii) Saul losing his sight on the road to Damascus (Acts 9: 1–19), (iii) Samson's story (Judges 16: 4–31).
5   Learn about the Festival of Light celebrated by Hindus and Sikhs called Diwali (an excellent book is O. Bennett, *Diwali* (Macmillan, 1986); see also second volume).
6   Learn about Hanukah — the festival of lights — celebrated by the Jews, a holiday when Jewish children receive presents, eat special food and light the eight-branched lamp, called the hanukiyah (see second volume).

Figure 6   *The Braille Alphabet*
(Reproduced by kind permission of the Royal National Institute for the Blind 224, Great Portland Street, London WIN 6AA).

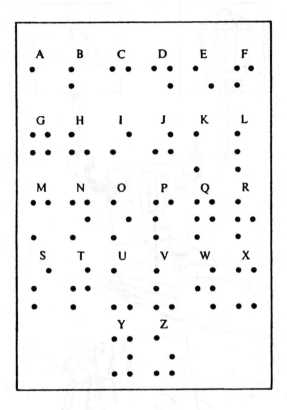

Science

A very useful book which is packed with simple scientific problems to solve is Ed Catherall, *Sight* (Wayland, 1981). Make a simple periscope with two mirrors and a tube, or make a book about optical illusions, (see Figures 7 and 8).

Art/Craft

1   Make a pair of green cellophane spectacles.
2   Experiment with light; try making shadow puppets.
3   Make a bird of prey mask, emphasizing the eyes.
4   Hang bird mobiles from the ceiling of the classroom.
5   Make a *rainbow disc* (see Figure 10).

Figure 7   Moving Pictures Are Optical Illusions

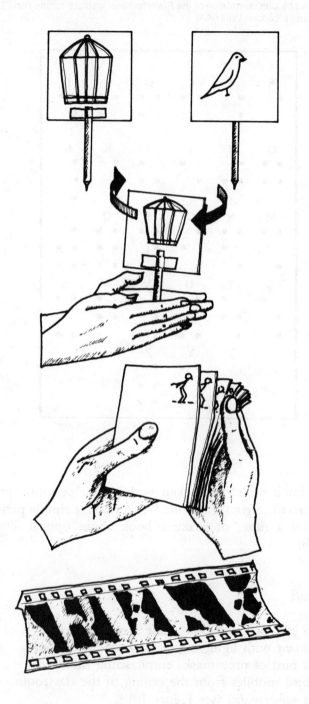

Figure 8   Optical Illusions

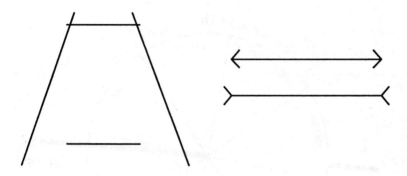

Figure 9   Make An Eye Colour Graph

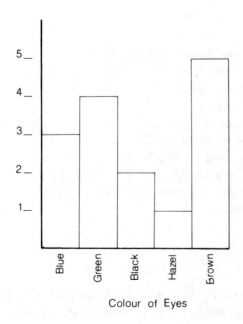

Colour of Eyes

Figure 10   How to Make a Rainbow Disc

1. Paint both sides of the cardboard.
2. Thread string through the centre.
3. Swing cardboard round, until the string is wound up.
4. Pull string tight and the spinning colours should merge and make white.

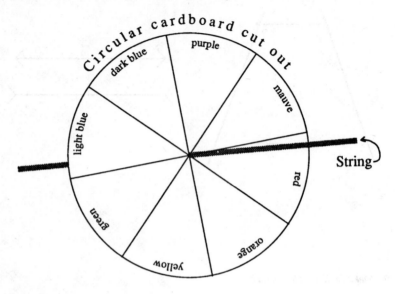

String

Resources

Books

CARWARDINE, M. *Night Animals* (Hamlyn, 1986).
JENSEN, V.A. and HALLER, D.W. *What's That?* (Collins, 1977) (this is a feely book designed primarily for blind children, but is also very interesting for sighted children).
KINCAID, D. and COLES, P. *Eyes and Looking* (Wheaton, 1981).
LAW, F. *Birds of Prey* (Collins, 1977).
MARTIN, G. *Owls* (A. and C. Black, 1980).
PETERSEN, P. *Sally Can't See* (A. and C. Black, 1975).
PLUCKROSE, H. *Look and See* (Franklin Watts, 1979).
Sight (Macdonald, 1984).

Poetry

The 'Magnifying Glass' by Walter de La Mare and 'The Eagle' by Alfred, Lord Tennyson in E. Blishe, *Oxford Book of Poetry for Children* (Oxford University Press). Reprint 1986.

The Eagle

He clasps the crag with crooked hands;
Close to the sun in lonely lands,
Ring'd with the azure world, he stands.

The wrinkled sea beneath him crawls;
He watches from his mountain walls,
And like a thunderbolt he falls.
Alfred, Lord Tennyson

Sight Assembly

Using all the ideas on (pp. 188–195), draw the information together as a whole and present an assembly. Children could read what they have researched and show what they have made.

Prayer

Heavenly Father, We do thank you for the miracle of sight. We take being able to see so much for granted that we cannot imagine what it must be like for those without sight. Help us to give generously to the Guide Dogs Association, so that others may 'see' through the eyes of their pets.

Hymn

No. 14, 'Who put the colours in the rainbow', in *Come and Praise* (BBC).

7–11
Activity/Assembly

Sound

The aim of this assembly is to help children to grow in awareness of themselves, i.e. to develop a positive attitude to life and learning.

Ephesians 2: 10 says, 'We are his handiwork.' To enable children to share in the wonder of God's handiwork, this assembly concentrates on the gift of hearing. The children might like to shut their eyes and consider the sounds that they can hear — sounds in the classroom, the street, the factory, the park, warning sounds, beautiful music, etc. In developing children's awareness and appreciation of this wonderful gift there is a need to help children to empathize with people who cannot hear. To join in the celebration of sound, the children might be encouraged to make their own musical instruments, compose a tune, or sing to the best of their ability in the school assembly.

Some scientific ideas have been suggested for the children to try for themselves. It is hoped that all these activities will develop a sense of wonder and awe.

Discussion Points

1 Discuss what sound is: anything that vibrates. Let the children experiment for themselves, e.g. with a ruler on a desk.
2 Discuss different kinds of sound in the street, in the country, in the home, in school, at night.
3 Talk about pleasant and unpleasant sounds, hard and soft sounds, decibel levels, warning sounds.
4 Discuss different sounds made by different musical instruments. Let the children make their own different instruments for themselves (See Figure 11 and books in 'Resources' section).
5 Talk about how sound travels, the speed of sound and echoes.
6 Discuss different voices, timbre and pitch; different languages, dialects, etc.; animal voices.
7 Talk about those who cannot hear, what it must be like to be deaf.
8 Be very quiet and still and listen to the sounds around about you.

Figure 11   How to Make Your Own Musical Instruments

Shakers

Washing up liquid bottles containing dried pulses.

Handles are made out of a piece of dowling rod inserted into the neck of the bottles and secured with strong stickly tape. Decorate the outside of the bottle.

Bells on Sticks

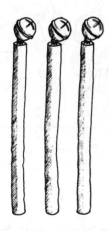

Small bells are nailed onto dowling rods and used as shakers.

Follow-up Activities for the Children

Written Work

Write about sounds you like to hear or sounds you don't like to hear.

Make a collection of sound words — 'babbling', 'murmuring', 'shouting', 'growling', 'crying', etc.

Write or retell a familiar story putting in sound effects.

Carry out research on the lives of some of the great composers and make a class book about them (see 'Resources' section for books to help you).

Learn the hand-signal alphabet (see Figure 12).

Figure 12   The Standard Manual Alphabet Card Published by the Royal National Institute for the Deaf 1990.
(Reproduced by kind permission of the RNID 105, Gower Street, London WC1E 6AH)

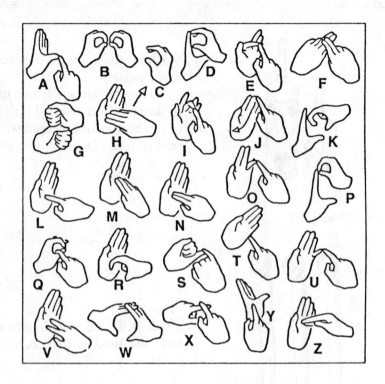

Religious and Moral Education

Helen Keller was deaf and blind and she was unable to speak because she could not hear any words or understand the need for them. Her teacher, Annie Sullivan, was determined to help Helen understand words by spelling them out on Helen's fingers. But Helen could not understand what Annie was doing, that is until ...

1   Lots of books recount the story of Helen Keller. It is simply told by F. Carr in *101 School Assembly Stories* Foulsham, 1973, but the part where Helen learns the meaning of W-A-T-E-R is beautifully retold by Margaret Davidson in R. Deadman and A. Razzell, *Awareness 2* (Macmillan, 1977).

> She now led Helen down to the old well-house that stood at the foot of the garden. Helen loved to play in its cool

dampness so now she scurried cheerfully inside. Annie took a deep breath and followed.

She began to bang the pump handle up and down, and soon a stream of water poured from its lip. She grabbed Helen's hand and struck it under the icy flow, and in the same instant began to spell W-A-T-E-R into the wet palm.

Helen went rigid and pulled widely toward freedom. But Annie held on. W-A-T-E-R ... W-A-T-E-R ... W-A-T-E-R, she drummed the word faster and faster into Helen's hand. Suddenly Helen stopped struggling. Or breathing. Or doing anything except concentrating on the shapes in her palm. W-A-T-E-R ... she felt the word burn down through her hand and into her brain. W-A-T-E-R, a light flooded across her face.

W-A-T ... she began to spell the word back to Annie. And with each movement of her own fingers, the namelessness retreated. She understood! These movements stood for the cool liquid that was pouring over her own hand! They always stood for that, and nothing else! She understood!

Source: M. Davidson in R. Deademan and A. Razzell, *Awareness 2* (Macmillan, 1977), p. 86.

2 Write to the Royal National Institute for the Deaf at 105 Gower Street, London WC1 6AH, or the National Deaf Children's Society at 45 Hereford Road, London W2 5AH, or find out if there is a unit for deaf children locally and see if a reciprocal visit could be made.

3 There is much good biblical material: (i) Jesus heals the deaf and dumb man (Mark 7: 31–37); (ii) the Old Testament Story of God calling Samuel (I Samuel 3); (iii) the Tower of Babel (Genesis 11: 1–9); there is a great idea for preparing for this, by talking in gibberish in various situations, in J. Gattis Smith, *Show Me*; Bible Society 1985 (iv) the psalms which are part of the Jewish worshipping tradition, e.g. Psalm 100, an excellent psalm to learn by heart and perhaps use in choral speaking at a school assembly; (v) the story of Gideon and the trumpets (Judges 6–8; and see Part 12, pp. 213–215).

Science

1 Make a simple telephone using two tin cans and a piece of string (See Figure 13).
2 Make a stethoscope using a piece of hosepipe and a funnel (See Figure 14).
3 Find out about the speed of sound (approx. 330 metres per second in air).
4 Find out about ultrasound, sonar and the doppler effect. (There are some useful books to help you in the 'Resources' section).
5 Find out about deaf children copying speech sounds by using a computer (See Figure 15).

Figure 13 Make Your Own Telephone

You will need two tin cans or plastic pots. Remove both ends and cover one end of each pot with tracing paper. Secure tracing paper with sticky tape. Thread a piece of string through each tin by making a hole in the tracing paper & securing the ends with knots or strong tape. Pull the string tight. One child talks into the can whilst the other child listens.

Music

Listen to some great classical pieces from Beethoven, Brahms, Chopin Mozart, etc. as well as folk music, pop music and jazz. Can you recognize the instruments being played?

Figure 14 Make Your Own Stethoscope

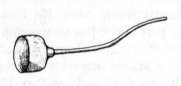

Cut the end off a plastic washing-up liquid bottle to make a funnel. Attach funnel to a length of hosepipe or plastic tube. One child holds the funnel against his chest, the other child listens, by placing the end of the tube to his ear.

Figure 15 Deaf Children learn to Speak Using a Computer

Deaf children speak into a microphone saying the word on the screen, until their speech patterns match those seen on the computer screen.

Resources

Books

FAMOUS COMPOSERS (Macdonald, 1969).
FAMOUS NAMES IN MUSIC (Wayland, 1979).
THE LIVES OF THE GREAT COMPOSERS, Books 1, 2, 3, (Ladybird, 1969).
ARDLEY, N. *Simply Science, Music and Sound* (Franklin Watts, 1984).
CATHERALL, E. *Hearing* (Wayland, 1981).
GATTIS SMITH, J. *Show Me: Practical Drama Techniques to Help 3–13 Year Olds Explore the Bible* (Bible Society, 1985).
GRIBBIN, M. *Hearing* (Macdonald, 1985).
KINCAID, D. and COLES, P. *Ears and Hearing* (Wheaton, 1981).
KOHN, B. *Echoes* (Wheaton, 1968).
Noises (Macdonald, 1973).
PETER, D. *Claire and Emma* (A. and C. Black, 1979) (contains photographs of children wearing hearing aids, yet leading a normal life).
SLOAN, C. *Helen Keller* (Hamish Hamilton, 1984).
WHITEHOUSE PETERSON, J. *I Have a Sister — My Sister Is Deaf* (Harper and Row, 1977).

Art/Craft

There are three books which are an absolute must for making musical instruments: M. Mandell and R.E. Wood, *Make your own Musical Instruments* (Sterling Publishing, New York, 1982) *The Musical Instrument Recipe Book* (Penguin, 1974); S. Dalby, *Make Your Own Musical Instruments* (Batsford, 1978).

Filmstrip

Our Senses, available from Philip Green Educational, 112a Alcester Road, Studley, Warwickshire B80 7NR. (tel.: 0527 854711).

Poetry

'Noise' in S. Mckellar, *My Family* (Evans).
Scannell, V. 'Intelligence Test' in S. McKellar, *Ourselves* (Macmillan).

Touch

For this assembly you will need some small home-made feely bags with draw-string tops that can be passed along the rows of children. Small items such as a marble, a rubber, a paper clip, a safety-pin, a crayon, a building brick, a piece of jigsaw, a bead can be placed in the bags. Children put their hands in the bags to feel what is inside; no peeping is allowed and no speaking to one's neighbour is permitted!

When the bags have traversed the hall, the teacher can ask the children to tell her, one at a time, what is inside. As the items are communicated to the teacher, she makes a list on a large sheet of paper pinned to an easel. When the remembered items have been said, the teacher can then tip everything onto a tray and match the children's guesses with the items that are revealed; discrepancies can be noted on the board.

The aim of this assembly is to show the children how much we rely on our sense of touch, when we are unable to use our eyes, and what a wonderful miracle this is. Draw out from the children that our hands can tell us many amazing things, such as when something is hot or cold, wet or dry, tight or slack, smooth or rough, hard or soft, clean or sticky, open or closed. The children should be encouraged to feel different surfaces and materials and learn something about the uniqueness of their finger tips and the prints they can make.

A class book could be constructed about all the different textures that we can feel such as sand-paper, velvet, bubbly material, and another book about all the things that we can feel by touching. Emphasize the need to use our hands in a kind and loving way, to touch others gently, never to harm, hurt or steal.

Tell the story of the woman who touched out for help, by touching the hem of Jesus' garment and was made well. Remind the children how we can touch for help or give help to others. (The story can be found in Matthew 9: 20–22, but is best told in the teacher's own words.) Emphasize that the woman knew that just touching Jesus would make her well, and that even though there were many people around him, Jesus knew who had touched him and that because of her faith, she was indeed healed.

There are many other stories about Jesus touching the sick and making them well. These stories could be told over a period of time: the blind man: John 9: 1–12; Jairu's daughter: Luke 8: 40–56; the man with the crippled hand: Luke 5: 12–16; Peter's mother-in law: Matthew 8: 14–15.

Prayer

Dear Lord Jesus, You healed the woman who was ill, when she just touched your garment. We thank you for the miracle of our sense of touch, and for our uniqueness and individuality. Help us never to use our sense of touch in an unkind way, but only for the good of others. Amen.

Hymn

No. 33, 'Jesus' hands were kind hands', in *Someone's Singing Lord* (A. and C. Black).

Taste

This assembly will need a little preparation beforehand. You will need four (or more) strips of sheeting to use as blindfolds for the volunteers, who will taste the distinctive tasting substances in various little pots, and enough clean spoons for each child taking part and for each pot. Substances such as strawberry jelly, marmite, peanut butter, cold baked beans, rice pudding can be used. You will need to choose four volunteers from the floor and blindfold them. Then you will need large stand-up labels describing the contents of each little pot after the tasting.

Marmite

The teacher passes along the line of volunteers with the spoons, to give a taste of each substance to each child, and then asks each child in turn to taste the substance, but not to say a word until the teacher has reached the last child. Then the teacher asks each child individually what they think they have just eaten. The labels can be arranged after all the children have had a guess. Then the teacher can turn to the assembly children after the first trial, and ask the children to correct any mistakes made by the volunteers, by looking at the substance and reading the labels. This exercise is repeated until all the substances have been tasted.

The teacher then needs to ask the volunteers to sit down and draw together the threads of the assembly. Mostly, the guesses of the volunteers will have been correct, and so the teacher can emphasize how fortunate we are to have this remarkable sense of taste. The teacher needs to raise the children's awareness of the wonder of taste that we have at our disposal: we can tell when something is sweet or savoury, good or bad, smooth or rough. The more exotic tastes of the world could be discussed. A large map of the world could be displayed and ribbons linking various dishes to the countries of origin could be shown.

Let the children imagine how they would feel if all their food tasted like cardboard, or paper or lettuce. Let some children shut their eyes and try eating pieces of lettuce, so that they can really imagine what a boring diet would be like.

End with a simple prayer of thanks for the variety of tastes. Perhaps parents from different ethnic groups could be invited into school to bring various dishes for the children to taste. Perhaps an Indian, Mexican or Chinese evening could be arranged for the next PTA meeting.

Prayer

Heavenly Father, We thank you for the wonderful tastes of the world. We are so grateful for this gift. Thank you too for all the different cultures of the world who produce such wonderful food for our enjoyment. Amen.

Song

'Food Glorious Food' from *Oliver*.

Smell

Screw-top bottles containing various strong-smelling liquids or substances are needed for this assembly. Child-proof medicine bottles are ideal for this purpose, not only to contain the substances, but also to remind the children of the dangers of tasting anything from bottles without labels or without the permission of adults. Tell the children how many young children die each year from tasting things they should not touch. Substances such as after-shave, tomato sauce, concentrated orange juice, cloves and mustard make ideal 'smells'.

Choose volunteers from the floor to come and sniff the contents of the bottles, not disclosing the real contents until many children have had a chance to guess. When lots of children have had a chance, reveal the contents of each bottle and label the bottle.

Allow children to make a book about their favourite smells. Perhaps children could paint a picture of the items that they love to smell. Encourage children to think of as many different smells as possible such as crackling bacon, hot chocolate, apple blossom, roses. Each child could make a list of their five best 'smells' and five things that they don't like to smell, such as bleach, cigarette smoke, rubbish tips.

Prayer

Dear Lord, We thank you, that with the gift of smell we have the remarkable ability to tell the difference between the beautiful scents of flowers and the dangers of bad chemicals. We know that some dangerous substances have no smell at all, so help us never to taste things without asking, in case we are harmed by them. Amen.

Hymn

No. 31, 'Thank you, Lord, for this new day', in *Come and Praise* (BBC).

12   Heroes and Heroines

5–11
Activity

Heroes and Heroines; Bravery and Courage

What makes a person one of the 'giants' of our society, like Mother Teresa, or Brother Andrew? It has something to do with a strong inner faith in God and when seeing a need, an overriding desire to do something about it. It has to do with perseverance, seeing a job through, going that extra mile. Jesus once said, 'If a man asks you to carry his bag one mile, carry it two miles' (Matthew 5: 41). The 'giants' of our society always go those extra miles, beyond physical and mental endurance.

Children need to see that these people started out as *ordinary* people doing an ordinary job well, and that the children too, can be 'giants' in their own school, in their home, in their community, by doing their work well, by truly seeking to serve others, or by standing up for their own beliefs.

Look back at the story of 'The Ugly Man' (pp. 124–6).

Discussion Points

1 Discuss why any man should risk his life for another.
2 Pick up the point that physical ugliness and coping with other people's rudeness takes a special kind of bravery.
3 Discuss men and women throughout history who have demonstrated enormous courage and bravery. Read some biographies of people such as Mother Teresa and discuss what motivates them (see further suggestions in the 'Resources' section).
4 Discuss people being imprisoned for their convictions, e.g. Nelson Mandela, and those willing to risk their lives for their faith, e.g. Brother Andrew, the Bible smuggler.
5 Finally, discuss where courage comes from: courage in little things leads to courage when it is really needed (see the story about the pilot below).

Follow-up Activities for the Children

Written Work

1 Write about a 'great life' in your own words (see 'Resources' list).
2 Write about a local person who has been especially brave.
3 Pretend you are a reporter. Write a report for the *'Daily News'* about an incident that actually happened in school. Or try and imagine what it was like at the trial of Jesus when his friends deserted him, and write a report.

Religious and Moral Education

1 Mother Teresa would often say, when helping lepers or children in war-torn areas, 'Let's do something beautiful for God.' Can the children think of something that they could do?
2 To teach the children about the RNLI, invite one of their speakers into school, or show the RNLI film and encourage the children to make a small collection. Two exciting true stories can be retold: (i) Henry Blogg, the coxswain of the lifeboat at Cromer, in Norfolk (this can be found in *Living Light*, Book 4 (Holmes McDougall, 1972); and (ii) Grace Darling, who rescued several people from the sea in a terrible storm (see pp. 221–3). One of these stories might be acted out for a school assembly.
3 Read the biblical stories about (i) Daniel's bravery: he continued to worship his God in spite of the King's command. (Daniel 6); it can also be read in C. Storr, *The Trials of Daniel* (Methuen, 1986); (ii) Paul's bravery in the storm at sea (Acts 27: 13–44); or (iii) the bravery of Jesus when he was captured, tried and sentenced to death (John 18, 19).
4 Remind the children of the courageous pilot whose engines failed over Chicago; how he thought of others before himself. He would not jump out of the plane because he knew the plane would crash onto many people, and he would not jettison the fuel because of the harm it would cause. He remained in the plane and with one chance only he brought the plane down safely.

Art/Craft

1 Make a painted portrait gallery of people who have shown out-standing courage or bravery including ordinary men and women.

2 Make a model of a lifeboat. Draw a large map of England and plot the RNLI stations around the English coast.
3 Make a frieze of the pilot and plane coming down over roof tops and trees to the runway.

Resources

Books

BENSON, M. *Nelson Mandela* (Hamish Hamilton, 1986).
LEIGH, V. *Mother Teresa* (Wayland, 1985).
PAVLAT, LEO, *Jewish Tales: The Eight Lights of the Hanukkiya* (Beehive Books, 1986) (this book contains many exciting stories of courage and bravery).
RICHARDSON, N. *Edith Cavell* (Hamish Hamilton, 1985).
RICHARDSON, N. *Martin Luther King* (Hamish Hamilton, 1983).
SPINK, K. *Gandhi* (Hamish Hamilton, 1984).
WALLINGTON, D. *Bible Smuggler: The Story of Brother Andrew* (RMEP, 1985).

5–11
Assembly

Gideon

This story of an Old Testament hero, an ordinary man who led his people to great victory, is told in Judges 6–8.

You will need the following characters:—

Gideon
Gideon's army (32,000 soldiers!)
    (cut-down squeezy bottles for trumpets)
    (small hand-held torches)
The Midianite army + cardboard swords

Tell the story in the following way. Long ago in the land of Israel there lived a young man called Gideon. There was great trouble at that time in the land where Gideon lived. People called the Midianites used to raid his people's farms and steal their sheep and cattle and all their grain. His people were called Israelites and they were very frightened of the Midianites. So they prayed to God for help.

One day, as Gideon was threshing wheat, an angel appeared to him and told him that God had chosen him to save his country from the Midianites. But Gideon was very surprised and said: 'How can I possibly save Israel? My family is poor and I am the youngest and least important member of my family!' But the angel promised that God would be with him.

When he was alone, Gideon became afraid; he knew that the Midianite army was much larger than the Israelite army and he was not at all sure that God would help him to defeat the Midianites. So Gideon prayed to God to give him a sign that God would help him. Gideon took a sheep's woollen coat, called a 'fleece', and put it outside on the ground that night. Then Gideon asked God to make the fleece wet with dew during the night, but leave the ground around the fleece dry. If God would do this, Gideon felt that he would know that God had chosen him to be the leader of the Israelite army.

The next day Gideon went outside and found that God had answered his prayer; the fleece was full of water, but the ground around the fleece was quite dry. But still Gideon doubted, and so he prayed to God once

more: 'Lord, do not be angry with me. I am still not sure that you want m
to be the leader of the people of Israel. Give me one more sign. This tim
may the fleece be dry and the earth around it be wet?'

The next morning when Gideon went to get the fleece it was perfectl
dry, although all around the fleece the ground was very wet with dew
This time Gideon was sure that God wanted him to be the leader. Gideo
called his army together. He gathered 32,000 soldiers. But God said t
Gideon: 'You have too many men. Tell all those who are afraid to go hom
and not to fight.' This time Gideon did as the Lord commanded, an
22,000 men returned home while 10,000 remained with Gideon. But Go
said: 'There are still too many men. Take all the men down to the river fo
a drink. Separate everyone who laps up the water with his tongue like
dog from those who get down on their knees to drink.' Three hundre
men scooped up water in their hands and lapped it like a dog; all the res
got down on their knees to drink. God told Gideon to keep the 300 me
who had lapped the water and to send the others home.

Gideon now had a very small army compared with the huge Midianit
army. For encouragement, God told Gideon to go down secretly to th
enemy camp. Gideon took his servant Purah with him. Outside one of th
tents Gideon and Purah overheard two men speaking. One man said, 'Las
night I had a strange dream. I dreamed a cake of barley bread tumbled int
the camp of Midian. It struck a tent and the tent overturned. I wonde
what it means?' His friend said in a frightened voice, 'It means God i
going to help Gideon to defeat us.' This gave Gideon the courage that h
needed. He prepared for battle. He divided his 300 men into three group
and gave each man a trumpet and a lamp covered by an earthenware pot t
hide the light inside. Gideon said to his men: 'Watch me and do exactly as
do. When we come to the edge of the Midianite camp blow your trumpet
on every side and shout: 'The sword for the Lord and for Gideon.'

In the middle of the night Gideon and his men marched towards th
enemy camp. Gideon blew his trumpet. All his men did the same and the
smashed their pots so that their lamps shone brightly in the darkness. The
held their torches in their left hands and their trumpets in their right hand
and shouted, 'A sword for the Lord and for Gideon.'

The enemy soldiers were so frightened when they heard all the nois
and saw all the bright lights that they ran away in fear and even fough
each other in their confusion. Gideon and his men chased the Midianit
army right out of the land. God had saved the people of Israel by usin
Gideon and just a few soldiers.

Then the people of Israel asked Gideon to be their ruler, but Gideo
replied, 'No, the Lord will rule over you.' At last there was peace in th
land while Gideon lived there.

Prayer

Father, Help us to trust you, just as Gideon trusted you. Guide us in all our plans great or small. Help us to know that you care for each one of us. Amen.

Hymn

No. 28, 'The Journey of life', in *Someone's Singing, Lord* (A. and C. Black).

7–11
Assembly

Sybil Phoenix: A Modern-Day Saint

(Based on an account by John Newbury in *Living in Harmony* (Religious and Moral Education Press, 1985).

Sybil Phoenix's life is an inspiration to everyone, boys and girls, black and white, young and old. This is a story of a black woman who has suffered much pain and distress because of her colour, but it is also the story of a woman who has achieved greatness through her love and dedication to God and his people.

It is suggested that the following main events of her life can be re-enacted by a class or group of children. She was born Sybil Marshall in British Guiana (now Guyana) in 1927. When she was only 9 her mother died and she went to live with her grandfather. She became a Christian and persuaded her grandfather to allow her to be confirmed. Her grandfather died only two years later and she went to live with her aunt and uncle, who did not really like her and treated her like a servant.

While she was still at school, Sybil helped at her church youth club. When she left school, she did a three-year evening class course to become a social worker. While running the youth club, she met Joe Phoenix, who was to become her husband. In 1956 Sybil and Joe came to England where they were soon married. Life was very hard for them. But Joe found work as a porter for an icecream company and Sybil went to work in a furniture factory. They found it very hard to find accommodation; to quote John Newbury's book, Sybil once saw a 'To Let' card which read 'No coloureds, no Irish, no dogs'. Today this would be illegal.

In 1962 Sybil and Joe moved to Lewisham with their two children, Lorraine and Trevor. The Methodist minister asked Sybil if she would help to run the church youth club. She readily agreed. Sybil and Joe's third child, Marsha, was born in 1964, and a year later Leticea was born. In 1965 a social worker asked Sybil and Joe if they would become foster-parents. They agreed, and many children found the love and security that they so badly needed in that loving home. John Newbury writes a moving account of their first foster-child, Tracy.

In 1967 another church youth club asked Sybil if she would help to run disco evenings for several hundred black youngsters. She agreed and when the club first opened, it was called the Telegraph Hill Youth Club. Later it was re-named 'Moonshot'. After moving from church hall to church hall permanent premises were eventually found in Pagnell Street, where Sybil

arranged classes in English, typing and accountancy for her black youngsters who often could not find jobs.

In 1972 Sybil was awarded the MBE for all her valuable work in the
community. A year later, in 1973, when Sybil was driving a group of
youngsters back from a beach holiday, she swerved to avoid a motor-
cyclist who was on the wrong side of the road and in the ensuing crash
Marsha, Sybil's daughter, was killed and Sybil herself was badly injured.
Sybil's faith in God was severely shaken, but she found the strength to go
on believing in Jesus as her friend, because of all the love that was shown to
her by black and white people alike.

The Pagnell Street Centre began to grow; more classes were arranged;
a mothers' project was set up; plans were made for an extension. In 1977
His Royal Highness the Prince of Wales visited the Centre at a time when
there was tension between the young people and the police. In December
1977 the Centre was burnt to the ground and Sybil was in despair, but not
for long. She persuaded the local authority to allow her to use an empty
church as a temporary youth club, and she started to raise funds all over
again to rebuild the centre. In addition, she raised the money needed to
open a hostel for foster-children, which was completed in 1979. She named
the hostel the Marsha Phoenix Hostel in memory of her lovely daughter.

In January 1981 tragedy struck again: a house in Deptford was set on
fire and thirteen young black people were killed. Sybil immediately went
to comfort the grieving parents and offered them her own home. She
raised money to help pay for the funerals of the young people. During this
time Sybil herself suffered much pain and insult from some people who
hated black people and who wanted to stop her work from flourishing.
Sybil often found her car tyres slashed, or paint poured over it, and she
received many obscene phone calls and threatening letters.

In March 1981 Prince Charles returned to open the new Pagnell Street
Centre. In November 1981 Sybil felt it was time to move on, so she
resigned as head of the Centre and went to work at a Methodist church in
Camberwell. She became director of MELRAW (Methodist Leadership
Racism Awareness Workshop), where she still works. She organizes
weekend courses and conferences to help people to understand that we all
belong to a world-wide family whatever the colour of our skin.

Prayer

Let us close with part of the prayer that Sybil herself wrote in 1984: 'Lord,
I know my charge is simple: to love and serve you, to keep faith, to spread
your loving kindness. Lord, give me the strength to continue in your
service. Amen.'

Song

End the assembly with the song: 'I'd like to teach the world to sing in perfect harmony' or a song from *'Mango Spice: 44 Caribbean Songs* (A. and C. Black) or No. 37, 'Working together', in *Every Colour under the Sun* (Ward Lock Educational).

At the end of his book of John Newbury gives some excellent practical suggestions for activities such as role play, a West Indian parents' evening, songs, folk tales, music and filmstrips as well as the following useful addresses:

MELRAW (Methodist Leadership Racism Awareness Workshop)
Director, Mrs Sybil Phoenix,
Clubland,
54 Camberwell Road,
London SE5.

who will arrange for a speaker (perhaps Sybil herself) to come and talk to a large group, school or church;

Commission for Racial Equality,
Information Department,
Elliot House,
10–12 Allington Street,
London SW1E 5EH.

for information about racial discrimination.
The book, **Living in Harmony**, is well worth buying. It includes many other useful addresses.

St Francis of Assisi

: was once said of St Francis of Assisi that he rolled in a pigsty to
·emonstrate his humility and obedience. Apparently he did this after Pope
·nnocent III had told him to go away and preach to pigs about living a life
f poverty like Jesus; this occurred in response to a request from St Francis
·r permission to form a new order of brothers. After first refusing, the
·ope was so impressed by Francis' humility and obedience that permission
·as granted. Francis gathered together some like-minded men, who
·anted to love and serve God by giving up all that they owned and move
·om village to village teaching the people about Jesus.

St Francis was not always poor and badly dressed. He was born about
·00 years ago, the son of a very rich silk merchant called Peter Bernardone.
·eter Bernardone gave his son plenty of money, fine clothes and lots of
·arties for his friends. But one day, on his way to fight in a war in
·outhern Italy, Francis met a courageous knight who was penniless and
·abbily dressed. Francis gave the man his own armour, feeling that the
·an deserved it more than he did, and he began to feel ashamed of the way
·at he had been living with so much wealth and good food to eat. He
·solved to give away all that he owned to the poor people around him. He
·ut on a coarse gown and tied it with a cord, and he went about the
·ountryside teaching and preaching about God, without even owning a
·air of shoes. He and his friends built some simple huts out of wood and
·ay in a little wood near a chapel just outside Assisi and formed the
·ompany of brothers that he had asked to form on that memorable occa-
·on. The brothers wanted only to serve God. They earned their food by
·orking in the fields for the local farmers.

One Christmas Francis and his friends re-enacted the story of the birth
·f Jesus, using live oxen, asses and sheep, and his friends acted as Mary and
·oseph and the shepherds. The villagers came from miles around to see this
·rst Nativity play and to understand, perhaps for the first time, the mean-
·g of Christmas.

In many ways the story of St Francis reminds me of our own Bishop
·eter of Lewes in Sussex. He too formed his own order of brothers called
·e Community of the Glorious Ascension, and pledged his life to serving
·sus and owning nothing but his clothes, although he does have a pair of
·oes! He too goes about the county supporting and talking to young and
·d people alike, and initiating caring and sharing projects. But his love for

mankind does not stop with the local people. In 1983 he started a special caring and sharing scheme that supports many overseas projects such as the Little Flower Leprosy Centre, Sunderpore, India, which provides medical attention and education for lepers; the Centre for the Rehabilitation of the Paralysed, Dacca, Bangladesh, which provides aid for the paralysed, including physiotherapy and teaching self-supporting skills such as weaving, printing and woodwork. Bishop Peter's similarity to St Francis does not stop with his life-style. He once turned a humble pigsty into a simple chapel in order to worship God in true humility and obedience.

Perhaps the children could find out more about charitable work overseas and initiate their own programme of support.

Prayer

Lord Jesus, Help us to be generous with our love, our time, our talents and our pocket money, to help those less fortunate than ourselves. Amen.

Hymn

No. 32, 'The hungry man' or No. 34, 'Would you turn your back?' in *Every Colour under the Sun* (Ward Lock Educational).

5–11
Assembly

Grace Darling

The following topic could form the basis of several assemblies spread over a number of days. Prior to the first assembly make a visit to the local or regional office of the RNLI to collect some excellent material for schools in order to set up an exhibition/display.

Give the children some statistics about the number of Royal Lifeboat Stations that there are around our coastal areas, and impress upon them that they are all manned by volunteers who depend upon our support. One of the RNLI films could be shown, or a collection made for RNLI funds, or pencils, badges and flags could be put on sale; or invite someone from RNLI to visit the school and describe their valuable work (see also p. 000).

Stress the enormous courage and bravery of crews who brave violent storms and fierce winds and waves to rescue boats in trouble. Perhaps attention could be drawn to a local rescue that has been reported in the newspapers, and a scrapbook could be made up about local heroes.

Finally, tell the story of the young girl, Grace Darling, who rescued several people from drowning after their ship had struck rocks in a terrible storm on the night of 6 September 1838. Grace Darling was born in 1815 in Northumberland in a small place called Bamburgh. Bamburgh was one of the first places to have a lifeboat station. But on this terrible night the storm was so bad that the lifeboat could not put out to sea.

You will need the following characters:

> Grace Darling
> Mother
> Father
> 9 survivors

If the whole class is to be involved in the assembly, the rest of the children could be divided into groups:

> Fierce waves (with crepe streamers
> Flowing from the children's wrists)
> The wind
> Rain
> Captain
> Crew
> 43 passengers

As the teacher/narrator tells the story, the children begin to mime their parts.

Narrator: Grace Darling lived with her mother and father in the Longstone Lighthouse off the Northumberland coast. Grace's father was the lighthouse keeper. [Enter father, mother and Grace.]

Narrator: One night there was a terrible storm. The waves rose up and battered against the rocks in a ferocious way. [Enter the waves and perform a raging, crashing movement, but remain in a 'frozen' pose as the story unfolds and each group acts its part.]

Narrator: The wind raged and blew the waves and tossed the foam high into the air. [Enter wind; four children rushing from each corner of the room makes an effective entrance and then 'freeze'.]

Narrator: The rain poured in torrents to join in a macabre dance of wind, rain and sea. [Percussion instruments and music can be played for this raging dance.]

Narrator: That very night on 6 September 1838 a steamer called the 'Forfarshire' was on the sea trying to make its way to safety, when suddenly it crashed onto vicious rocks and the ship was broken in half. [Enter captain and crew who try to steer the ship, passengers cling to each other for safety; then with a crash of cymbals, the ship breaks up and everyone is flung into the water. Forty-three passengers are drowned and covered by the waves; nine cling to the wreck.]

Narrator: Grace woke early that morning, unable to sleep because of the storm, but as she lay listening to the storm, she heard other sounds, desperate cries for help. She leapt out of bed and shouted to her father that there must be a wreck outside. Peering through the mists and gloom, she suddenly caught sight of the wreck and the poor people clinging to it. [Grace mimes the actions.]

Narrator: She begged her father to fetch their small fishing boat to rescue the people. But her father sadly shook his head, telling her that it was impossible to reach the people in such a terrible storm. He reminded her that even the Bamburgh lifeboat had not been able to brave those fearful waves. [Grace and her father mime this conversation.]

Narrator: But Grace made up her mind to go alone and try to save those poor people. When her father saw that she was determined to go, he relented and agreed to help her. They set out across the raging sea, tossed and turned in every direction, while they rowed with all their strength and might. [The two row; wind, waves and rain buffet and batter them.]

Narrator: They struggled desperately until they reached the nine people who were still alive. Somehow they managed to get five of them into their little boat, and they made the gruelling return journey. [Mime the actions.]

Narrator: Mrs Darling helped the survivors out of the boat and into the lighthouse, made them hot drinks, warmed them around the fire and gave them blankets to revive their frozen bodies. [Mime the actions.]

Narrator: Mr Darling and two of the men that they had saved made the terrifying return journey once more to pick up the remaining four survivors. [Actions are mimed.]

Narrator: The news of Grace's courage and bravery soon spread throughout the country, and both she and her father were awarded gold medals for their readiness to risk their own lives in order to save others.

Prayer

Heavenly Father, We ask your blessing on all those brave people who go out to sea to risk their own lives in order that others may live. Amen.

Hymn

No. 26, 'When lamps are lighted in the town', in *Infant Praise* (Oxford University Press).

5–11
Assembly

<hr>

St Paul

<hr>

Read I Corinthians 9: 24–25; *Good News Bible*: 'Surely you know that many runners take part in a race, but only one of them wins the prize. Run, then, in such a way as to win the prize. Every athlete in training submits to strict discipline, in order to be crowned with a wreath that will not last; but we do it for one that will last for ever.' (Quotation from the Good News Bible, published by the Bible Society/Collins is reproduced with the permission of the publishers).

Paul was writing to the Church at Corinth when he compared the Christian endeavour to the strict training of an athlete. Many assemblies could be based on the sayings and life of St Paul. This saying has been chosen to demonstrate a simple example.

Find a large picture of an athlete. (*Athletics Weekly* published by World Athletics and Sporting Publications Ltd, 342 High Street, Rochester, Kent ME1 1ED could help.) Daley Thompson would be a good choice because he is a decathlete and trains for ten events. Ask ten children to paint the different events: 100 metre sprint, long jump, shot-put, high jump, 400 metre run, high hurdles, throwing the discus, pole-vault, throwing the javelin, 1500 metre run; and display the paintings in a circular fashion around the picture of Daley Thompson.

On large pieces of card, in large letters for all to see, write down the following words: 'self-discipline', 'perseverance', 'patience', 'love', 'joy', 'peace', 'kindness'. Explain the meaning of each word, or ask the children for their own explanation, and tell the children how Daley demonstrates these qualities. The following list is one way:

self-discipline — by training hard on a regular basis;
perseverance — trying harder when he has failed;
patience — waiting his turn, being patient with others;
love — love of his sport, love of life, love for fellow athletes;
joy — the joy he gives other people and his own joy when he succeeds;
peace — the peace he finds in doing the sport he loves best;
kindness — how he helps other athletes and encourages them.

Let seven other children place the word cards underneath the paintings, and ask the children to think of *other* qualities that could be written underneath the remaining paintings.

Draw the assembly to a close by reminding the children of the words at the beginning, and explain that every child may not win a gold medal for ten events, but at least every child can strive for excellence in one personal or academic area of the curriculum, e.g. kindness to each other or excellence in sport or scientific studies. Remind the children that it is not winning that counts but trying one's best, and not the prize that matters but achieving everlasting personal qualities.

Prayer

Father, We ask you to help each one of us to do our best for your sake. Amen.

Hymn

No. 48 'Do your best', in *Every Colour under the Sun* (Ward Lock Educational).

5–11
Assembly

Elijah's Story

This Old Testament story about worship, based on I Kings 17, 18, can b
rehearsed briefly before the assembly or can be read aloud (giving direc
tions as necessary) without any rehearsal at all. It has been found to wor
as well with top juniors as with infants, as the humour appeals to all age
alike.

The version of the story is best read from Joann Scheck, *The Water th*
Caught on Fire (Arch Book 1969). If the rhyming version is disliked, othe
words can be substituted with ease, without destroying the humour.

The characters can be chosen from the assembled school:
They are:—

> King Ahab
> Queen Jezebel
> Elijah
> 4 Ravens
> 450 Priests of Baal (10 children will actually do!)
> 4 jar carriers

The outline of the story is as follows: Queen Jezebel persuades Kin
Ahab to build a temple to a new God made of stone (both bow down an
pray). Elijah warns the pair that if they go on praying to the stone Goc
Baal, his true God would hold back the rain for three years, and everythin
would die. [Enter Elijah, who wags a forefinger in warning.]

God keeps his promise and everything dies. However, he show
Elijah a natural spring, where he can get plenty of water, and he sends fou
ravens to feed him every day. [Four ravens flap around the hall looking fc
food and return to feed Elijah.]

Elijah returns to King Ahab and challenges him to put the King's nev
God, Baal, to a test of power with his own true God. The King agrees, an
all the people are summoned to Mount Carmel, together with 450 priest
of Baal. [The priests of Baal line up and are given their marching orders b
a leader — they march around the hall.] Elijah commands the 450 priests c
Baal to collect sacks of wood and build a high altar. He challenges th
priests to ask Baal to consume the wooden altar with fire. [The priest
collect wood and build the altar; the teacher can enter into the fun b
telling the children to work harder and find more imaginary wood.]

Then the priests perform their prayer-dance. [They dance and they op all round the altar, until they drop, but nothing happens.] Elijah stands p and says that it is his turn, but that wood is too easy for his God to urn, so he fetches twelve big stones. [The rest of the children can help lijah by counting to twelve as Elijah picks up the imaginary stones.] Then lijah digs a deep trench around the stones. [The teacher can tell Elijah to ut a bit more effort into the digging.]

lijah commands four men to fill four large jars of water to throw over the vood and thoroughly drench it. He tells them to do it again, three times. inally, Elijah kneels and prays that God will burn up the altar to show that Ie is the one true God.

The teacher needs to quieten the hall as she explains that a great flame oared out of the sky and burned the wood and stones and even the water. 'he people and priests fall silent and then kneel on the ground and promise) worship the one true God.

Prayer

Ve thank you for the courage and bravery of Elijah; for his fearlessness to peak out when others followed man-made Gods. May we also have this ourage. Amen.

Hymn

Io. 61, 'Praise to the Lord, the Almighty, the King of Creation', in *New ife* (Galliard).

5-11
Assembly

St Margaret

This story can be mimed by a class of children. Special days and saints days can be remembered throughout the year. A simple assembly can b drawn from the life of a saint such as St Margaret, who was a real princess You will need the following characters:

Princess
called Margaret
brother
Prince Edgar
sister
Princess Christina
oarsmen
King Malcolm
church builders
eight children
school children
mothers
poor
sick and needy people

Simple costumes can be worn. Crowns for the King and Queen and ragge clothes for the poor, etc.

One child reads the following story, while the other children mime th actions. A princess called Margaret sailed from England to Scotland wit her brother Prince Edgar and sister Princess Christina. [The princes brother and sister mime getting into a boat; the oarsmen begin to row King Malcolm of Scotland welcomed the family and he fell in love wit Princess Margaret. Later he married Margaret. She became his Queen. [. crown is placed on her head.]

They built a church in Dunfermline to thank God for their happine [Six or eight church builders mime sawing, hammering, building, etc They had eight children. [Eight children enter and sit at the King an Queen's feet.] Queen Margaret used to read stories to the children. [Sl mimes reading a story.]

Every day Margaret prayed to God to ask him how she could help h new people, the people of Scotland. [Margaret quietly kneels and shuts h eyes to pray.] She began to open schools where children could learn to read and write. [Enter children to sit crossed-legged and pretend to write.] She taught mothers how to make clothes for their children. [Enter some mothers with material; Margaret makes large sewing movements; the mothers copy.] Every day the castle doors were opened to the poor, the sick and the needy. [Mime doors being opened, beggars enter limping, with bandages around their heads, arms, etc. Margaret gives each a bowl of food to eat.]

The people of Scotland loved Queen Margaret very much because she was so good and kind to everyone. She did all these things because she loved God so much.

Prayer

Thank you for the lives of ordinary men and women, boys and girls, who, inspired by their great love for you, are enabled to achieve great things for others. Amen.

Hymn

No. 63 'Sing Hosanna', in *New Life* (Galliard).

7–11
Assembly

St George, St Patrick, St Andrew and St David

The children could make the appropriate flags for each saint and join them together at the end of the assembly to form the 'Union Jack'. Dramatize an incident in the life of each saint, using puppets. This assembly is not intended for very young children. Some understanding of myth and legend is needed before proceeding.

St Andrew

The patron saint of Scotland and commemorated on 30 November.

Flag

An X-shaped white cross on a blue background which forms part of the 'Union Flag'.

Dramatic Incident

St Andrew was one of the first disciples to follow Jesus. His brother was called Simon Peter. They were fishermen. [Dramatize the call of the fishermen.] The legend explaining why St Andrew is the patron saint of Scotland is thought to be this. After Jesus died Andrew travelled far and wide, teaching the people about God. He was put to death in Greece on a cross shaped like a letter 'X'. A priest called Regulus brought St Andrew's bones back from Greece to Scotland. The town where his bones are now thought to be buried is called St Andrews.

St Patrick

The patron saint of Ireland and commemorated on 17 March.

Flag

An X-shaped red cross on a white background which forms the second part of the 'Union Flag'.

Dramatic Incident

St Patrick is supposed to have rid Ireland of snakes. The last snake was very difficult to catch, but St Patrick tricked the snake by asking it to prove how it could fit into a small box; once it was inside, St Patrick tossed the box into the sea. Once, when St Patrick was preaching, he picked a shamrock to teach the people about the 'oneness' of God the Father, God the Son and God the Holy Spirit. Now Irishmen all over the world wear a shamrock on St Patrick's day.

St George

The patron saint of England and commemorated on 23 April.

Flag

A red cross on a white background which forms the final part of the 'Union Flag'.

Dramatic Incident

This is the legend that was told of St George. The people of a town in North Africa lived in great fear of a dragon. Every day the dragon ate one of the people, and one day the King's own daughter had to be the next victim. St George rode up on his horse and killed the dragon and saved the princess. He claimed that Almighty God had given him the power to defeat the dragon and so the people should thank God for their deliverance.

Union Flag

Now make the Union Jack flag. First lay down the white diagonal cross on a blue background of St Andrew. Over this lay the red diagonal cross of St Patrick. Over these place the upright cross of St George. Together these three flags make up the Union Jack.

St David

The patron saint of Wales and commemorated on 1 March.

Flag

A white dove with a golden halo; a green mount; all on a silver background.

Dramatic Incident

One legend tells us that there were once some people who began to spread false stories about God. So David spoke the truth to a large crowd of people. As he was speaking, a white dove appeared and settled on his shoulder, and the ground where he was standing rose up, so that he could be seen as well as heard. The people were so amazed that they went away cured of their false beliefs. David travelled about Wales, teaching the people about God. He built monasteries where the monks grew their own food. Today Welsh people often wear a leek on St David's day in remembrance of him.

Prayer

Lord Jesus, Help us to be brave and courageous, honest and truthful, like the saints of old. Amen.

Hymn

No. 34 'When a knight won his spurs', in *'Someone's Singing Lord'* (A. and C. Black).

7–11
Activity

A Child of Courage

If we are really honest, most of us lack courage at some time or another. There is a need to bring children to understand that they cannot always be brave. There will be times when they lack the courage to take the appropriate action, to speak out against injustice, to fail to tell the truth. But having recognized this, there is a need also to develop a sense of inner courage; to ask God's help for the right kind of courage at the right time; to speak the truth. It needs to be emphasized that if children have courage to do little things, then when it really matters, they will have the courage to do great things.

Discussion Points

We are going to talk about courage and bravery today. What does courage or bravery mean to you? Of course, it will mean different things to different people.

1 Do you remember the children who were crippled for life by a sniper's bullet in Beirut? They came to England, a foreign country to undergo painful surgery and they had to learn to walk with artificial limbs without understanding a word that was said to them. That is what I call bravery.

2 And what about the ordinary girl whose mum and dad have divorced, and the girl has had to adjust to new situations, perhaps looking after younger brothers and sisters, perhaps living in a new house, with a new mother or father — that takes courage too.

3 Think about telling the truth, or owning up after an incident in school — that takes real courage. Or what about protecting someone in the playground from a bully, or stopping a fight or an argument, or stopping someone from mistreating a dog. All these things take courage to act on or to speak out about, or to do, without being told by someone else. (See the poem about being brave on page 236–7).

Discuss different types of bravery:

4 Physical bravery — saving someone who is drowning; helping someone who is being attacked; brave children who are in physical

pain; brave men and women who are in tough jobs — firemen, lifeboatmen, bomb-disposal experts, special air servicemen — all those who risk their lives for others.

5   Spoken bravery — the courage to say 'No' to stealing, lying, drugs; to speak out against injustice against other people; or to stop animals being mistreated.

6   The courage to make the 'right' decision.

Divide the children into groups and try some role playing situations. For example, it is time for assembly; the headmaster has told the children that it is imperative for everyone to be there; everyone is getting ready to go into the hall, when one of the children brings in a bird with a broken wing; what should the class do?

Follow-up Activities for Children
Written Work

1   Make a scrap book about the 'Children of Courage' awards.
2   Invite the children to research this topic in the local library.
3   Encourage the children to write about their own brave moments.
4   Compile a Zig-zag class book.

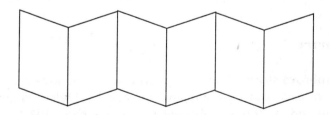

Religious Education

1   As a class or school project, sponsor a child in the Third World. Sponsorship information, filmstrips and posters are available from Tearfund, 11 Station Road, Teddington, Middlesex TW11 9AA (Tel: 081977 9144).

2   Support a children's hospice.

3   For physical bravery, read the story of David and Goliath in the *Good News Bible* (1 Samuel 17: 1–58.)

4   This chapter also includes David's own account of how he protected his father's sheep from wild animals (see verses 34–37).

5 For verbal bravery, read the story about the little slave girl who was not afraid to speak out and so saved her master, Captain Naaman, from certain death. II Kings 5: 1–19; see also p. 152 above).

6 Recall the story of Esther, the Jewish girl who saved her people (read the book of Esther in the Old Testament).

Music

1 'One more step along the world I go', in *Come and Praise* (BBC 1978).

2 'Two little boys' by Rolf Harris.

Art/Craft

1 Goliath was 'six cubits and a span high' (approximately 10 feet tall 1 Samuel 17: 4). Encourage the children to measure in hand span and cubits, and make a collage of Goliath and David.

2 Paint action pictures of bravery, e.g. a fireman rescuing a person from a blazing building, or a swimmer saving someone who is drowning.

3 Design a poster saying 'No' to drugs.

Resources

Read the humorous story of three boys who were not so brave, but found courage in each other's company, written by Dylan Thomas, in R Deadman and A. Razzell, *Awareness 2* (Macmillan, 1977).

LEIGH VANORA, *Anne Frank* (Wayland, 1985) is an excellent factual account of this brave girl, written for junior school children. It contains some excellent original photographs and line drawings as well as an exciting story.

Also see P. FRANK, *Queen Esther Saves Her People* (Lion Publishing, 1986).

INNOCENTI R., *Rose Blanche* (Jonathan Cape, 1985) is a lovely story, set a the time of World War II, of a child who discovers some Jewish children in a concentration camp, close to her home, and feeds them from her own food. It contains beautiful pictures, sensitively drawn; a story of a brave girl with a very sad ending (intended for 7-9-year-olds).

Bravery

Sometimes you can see bravery,
Like when a man
Pulls a small boy out of the road
To save him from a car.
Or on television
In a film about battles
When the soldiers go forward
To fight and perhaps be wounded.
Or you can hear it —
Hear being brave,
When a boy in the park shouts
'I'm not afraid, I'll climb that tree!'
or 'fight that boy',
or 'play that trick'.
> But sometimes bravery doesn't show.
> You get a feeling, right inside,
> You feel screwed up,
> Afraid and
> Frightened.
> Being brave is when you face it,
> Whatever you're afraid of.
> It's when you say, 'I'll do it',
> Or 'I'll go', or 'I don't mind'.
If you've never been brave
You won't know what I mean.
But if you have
You'll smile and feel warm,
— And you'll be ready
To be brave again.

A. Farncombe, *It's Our Assembly* (NCEC, 1979).

7–11
Assembly

The Unknown Boy Hero

(Adapted for radio by Elizabeth Peirce from the story 'People aren't always what they seem', in R.H. Lloyd, *Assemblies for School and Children's Church* (Religious Education Press Limited, 1974.)

This story is about a very brave boy who, although he was in great pain, always thought of others before himself. There was once a boy who was very ill indeed. He was taken to hospital and admitted to a very tiny ward with only two beds in it. His bed was placed next to the window and there was an empty bed placed next to the wall. He was known as 'Smiley', because he was always cheerful, even though he was so ill.

One night another young boy called Kevin was brought into the hospital and he was placed in the empty bed beside the wall. As both boys were very ill, all they could do was talk to each other. So day by day the boy Smiley, who was placed next to the window, would describe to Kevin everything that he could see from his window. He described the birds, the flowers, the trees and the shops; and often he would make Kevin laugh by describing the people and the antics of a dog chasing a cat and so on.

Although Kevin loved hearing about what was going on outside, secretly he was very jealous of Smiley being by the window. He envied Smiley's view, and he wished that he too could look out and see all that was going on. So he asked the nurse several times if he could swap beds with his friend, but somehow nothing was ever done about it. As the months went by Smiley continued to amuse Kevin by describing the world outside. He tried to take the other boy's mind off his pain and suffering.

One night Smiley was removed to another hospital for more intense treatment. So when Kevin saw the empty bed by the window, he asked the nurse again to move him next to the window. This time his request was granted. With great excitement he looked out of the window. But all he could see was a blank wall and two dustbins. Suddenly, he realized that the other boy had imagined all that he saw for his benefit, to try and cheer him up and keep him happy and to take his mind off the pain.

The boy by the window had great courage, didn't he? How easy it would have been for him to grumble about being in hospital, or to moan about his illness. But what did he do? He didn't think about himself at all, or his own problems. He turned all his attention and his imagination to cheering up the other boy. He made up funny stories about different characters just to help to take the other boy's mind off his pain and to make him laugh. Now that takes real bravery. Could you be that brave if you were ill?

Prayer

Father, Help us to be like the boy in the story, always ready to cheer up someone else and to think of others rather than ourselves. Amen.

Hymn

No. 43, 'Stick on a smile', in *Every Colour under the Sun* (Ward Lock Educational) or No. 10, 'Poor child', in *Tinderbox: 66 Songs for Children* (A. and C. Black).

13 Twenty Quick Assemblies

**5–11
Assemblies**

Twenty Quick Assemblies/'Life Savers'
---

1   *Words*

Each day write a different word on a card to discuss or to think about: e.g. 'Happiness is ...', 'Love is ...', 'Sympathy', 'Truth', 'Forgiveness', 'Bricks', 'Steps', 'Hopes', 'Fears'.

2   *An ABC of 'Thank You's'*

Each day take a different letter of the alphabet: a thank-you day for apples, aunties, ants, etc.

3   *Famous Composers and Different Musical Instruments*

Introduce a different piece of music each day and talk about the composer or show a different musical instrument and find a piece of music to illustrate its use. Give thanks for this wonderful gift.

4   *Famous Artists*

Ask the museum service to loan various paintings and tell the children something about the artist and his life. Encourage children to collect postcards and old Christmas cards by famous painters. The Ladybird publishers produce a very useful series of books under the title Great Artists.

5   *Colours (for Infants)*

If there has been too much passive listening, then introduce some active participation by having a colour dance: all the children wearing something red dance to this music (be sure to have rules like 'sit down very quickly when you hear the tambourine!'). Then all the children wearing different colours dance to this music, etc. Or have a green, orange, blue, day, when children think of things with these colours. End with a simple prayer of thanks to God.

6   *Patterns*

There are patterns in everything. Look at drain-hole covers, roof-tops, gates, shoes, jumpers, etc. Find as many patterns as you can. Make a list, ask children to get their parents to help at home. (Be prepared for infants to think of a pattern long after the assembly has terminated!)

7   *Marionettes/Puppets*

In a moral play puppets can do and say things that children should not do or say. If you pull the strings of a marionette, you can do things like kick and punch. Tell the children that there is no one pulling their strings, and that they can control their feet and hands and tongues!

8   *Visits*

Capitalize on all visits made by children to zoos, bird sanctuaries, dolphinariums, museums, etc. Ask them to describe what they saw or show the kind of movement that the animals or birds made. End with a simple prayer of thanks to God.

9   *After School I . . .*

Encourage children to share their hobbies after school, e.g. swimming, ballet, football, chess, stamp collecting, knitting, cooking. Help them to describe their hobby, and foster the interest of other children who perhaps do not have a hobby. This will encourage all children to lead richer and fuller lives.

10   *Light*

Think of all the things we can do in the light. What do we need light for? Where does it come from? How many different ways can light be brought into our homes or schools? Link with Jesus as the 'Light of the World.'

11   *Darkness*

Think about the different activities that we do at night. Think about sleep, going to bed routines, night workers. What do birds and animals do at night? Do they all sleep? Think about those that hunt at night.

12   *God's Beautiful World*

Encourage the children to be interested in everything, e.g. flowers, leaves, cobwebs, insects (always remembering to return any insects to their natural habitats).

13   *Favourite Things*

Have a day for bringing your favourite thing to school, e.g. teddy bears. Space and weather permitting, have a teddy bears picnic assembly.

14   *Space*

Listen to *The Planets* by Gustav Holst. It is suitable for movement and dance. Think about the wonder of outer space. Collect pictures and books for display. Imagine what it would be like to move in space, to blast off and to land in space; to collect rocks and rare specimens. A group of children could build themselves into a weird planet structure or move like an astronaut.

15   *Pop Music*

Use popular records such as *Memories* by Barbara Streisand or *Two Little Boys* by Rolf Harris as a starting point for a particular theme. Play the whole record, then ask the children about their feelings, attitudes and responses.

16   *Books*

Many fiction books provide excellent starting points to discuss a moral question, e.g. D. Edwards *My Naughty Little Sister* (for Infants), especially the story where my naughty little sister picks up the workmen's food. This

244

raises all sorts of questions about touching things that do not belong to oneself. Or read *Dogger* by Shirley Hughes, which raises the issue of selflessness and generosity. Scripture Union publishes many explicitly Christian, brightly coloured books that can be enjoyed for their own sake or the 'message' that they are trying to convey.

17   Poetry

Reading a meaningful poem often speaks more to children than many prepared talks. Some discussion and a time of quiet reflection is needed.

18   News

Various children come out and speak for a very few minutes about their news, helped and prompted by the teacher, who closes the service with a prayer that embodies all the things that have been talked about. (Be prepared for a variety of topics from seeing dead cats to visiting grandma.)

19   Choose

Volunteers come out and choose their favourite hymn from a wide selection of hymn books. They can also choose some friends to help with percussion accompaniment. (This may need to be controlled or conducted, if the children get carried away with enthusiasm!) End with a simple prayer of thanks for the message and the joy of singing and making music.

20   Views

Think of a subject and ask if anybody would like to come out and talk about it, or allow the children, to suggest a topic. Break into smaller groups around the hall. Teachers could go around the groups (it is useful if you have students to help, and be prepared for discussion 'noise'). One such idea came from a child: 'What is God really like?' All the ideas were honestly fed back to the headteacher, including such thoughts as 'an old man in the sky with a beard', but it was decided to adopt the one 'He is like Jesus; like Father, like Son. We look like our parents.'

14 Background Information for Teachers

Foundation of the Faiths

Christianity

Background Information

Symbol of the Cross.   Christians believe there is only one God Almighty. He is known and worshipped in three parts: God the Father, God the Son, God the Holy Spirit. The cross has become the symbol of Christianity as a reminder that God sent his son Jesus Christ to be crucified on a cross to be the perfect sacrifice for the sins of the world.

Jesus Christ.   God's son. He was born in Bethlehem, 2000 years ago. Jesus means 'God saves'. Christ means 'The anointed one'. Mary, his mother, was a virgin; Joseph, his 'father', was carpenter. Christians believe that Mary was chosen by God to bear his son as fulfilment of the promise made to the Jews in the Old Testament. Jesus grew up in Nazareth, and started his ministry when he was 30 years old. You can read about his birth and life in the Gospels of the New Testament of the Holy Bible.

Holy Bible.   Christians believe this Holy Book was inspired by God. It is divided into two parts, the Old and the New Testaments. The first part tells the history of the Jewish people and the promise of the Messiah (the anointed one); the second tells about Jesus, His life and teachings, His miracles and parables. It also contains the letters Jesus' followers wrote to each other after his death.

Christians.   Roman Catholics, Church of England, Methodist, Salvation Army, Baptist, Congregational, Church of Scotland, United Reform, Pentecostal, Quaker, Orthodox are all Christians who have the same fundamental belief that Jesus Christ was the son of God, but they differ slightly in their particular beliefs and manner of worship (see pp. 254–8).

Worship.   Christians worship God in many different ways; through singing, praying, praising, thanking God, going to church and dedicating their lives (like nuns and monks and missionaries). They try to obey God's commandments in the Old Testament and follow the teaching of Jesus Christ in the New Testament. Christians attend church every week, and believe that Christianity is a way of life, that they belong to the worldwide family of God. Therefore, worship is not confined to Sundays only, but Christians pray each day, read their Bibles, attend prayer meetings and Bible study groups during the week, as well as care for others and give to charities.

Family Life

Christian Family Life

Background Information

Baptism. In the Church of England babies are baptized or Christened. In some of the free churches baptism occurs when people are old enough to make the decision to become Christians for themselves (see pp. 256–8).

Confirmation. Each Christian faith has a different age for its children to confirm their faith (see pp. 254–9). In the Church of England confirmation occurs at about the age of 13 years. A young person must attend confirmation classes and come to profess the Christian belief for himself. He is the confirmed by the Bishop and is able to receive Holy Communion. This is the regular service of sharing bread and wine in remembrance of Christ's body and blood that was shed for the forgiveness of sins.

Sunday. This is the day of rest for all Christian people. Many Christians believe that no work should be done on this day (apart from essential services like the work of running hospitals, homes for the elderly or for children, etc.).

Junior Church. Many Christian children attend Sunday School, or special classes especially for young people; often they will join the grown-ups at a family service and might even present the worship themselves.

Choir. Many churches have a choir of boys and girls, men and women, who meet together to practise songs and play musical instruments each week to enhance the Sunday worship. Guitars, hand-bells, recorders, tambourines are all used, as well as many other musical instruments.

Minister. In different churches the spiritual leader of the church has different names such as 'priest', 'rector', 'father', 'vicar', 'elder', 'clergyman' and 'chaplain'. In some cases they wear special clothes as a sign of their calling and responsibility. They conduct the services and preach or teach the people in their congregation. They have many duties such as marrying people, taking funerals, visiting the sick or elderly, teaching Bible classes, attending meetings to do with church finance and buildings, visiting schools and leading youth groups.

Food. The Lord's Supper or Holy Communion is commemorated in remembrance of Jesus Christ's last meal with his disciples before his death. It consists of eating bread and drinking wine (read Luke 22: 14-20). Other special food is connected with the Christian festivals: for instance, Christians eat special festive food at Christmas, the celebration of the birth of Jesus Christ. They also give each other Easter eggs on the third day of Easter (Sunday) as a symbol of Jesus' resurrection or new life.

Christian Festivals

Find out about the special Christian festivals. Compile a topic book on the following.

Easter. This festival takes place in the spring. It is the most important Christian festival. Jesus Christ's death and resurrection are commemorated.

Good Friday. Christians remember how Jesus was tried, mocked, tortured and crucified on this day. Some churches hold services lasting for three hours, in remembrance of the final three hours that Jesus hung upon the cross and the sky turned black from 12 o'clock until he died at 3 o'clock (see Luke 23).

Easter Sunday. On this day Jesus rose from the dead; a joyful day for Christians everywhere (read Luke 24). The churches are decorated with many flowers. Special hymns of thanks and praise are sung. Many churches build a garden tomb with the stone rolled away as a reminder of the empty tomb in Jerusalem where Jesus was buried.

Lent. This is the forty days before Easter. Christians remember this as the time that Jesus fasted and was tempted by the Devil in the desert before he started teaching. In remembrance of this Christians often try to fast or to give up something they particularly like during Lent. The money saved is then given to charity.

Palm Sunday. This was the time of the Jewish Passover when Jesus rode into Jerusalem and was hailed as King. It is commemorated today on the Sunday before Easter. Some churches give crosses to their congregation made out of palm leaves, in remembrance of this.

Advent. The four weeks before Christmas are called 'Advent' (or 'the coming').

Christmas. The celebration of the birth of Jesus Christ. Many churches and schools re-enact the scene at the time (as described in Luke 2).

Whitsun. This festival is sometimes called 'Pentecost' (the Greek word meaning fiftieth) because it was the festival celebrated by the Jews called 'Shavout' fifty days after the Passover festival. Today Christians remember this day as the day when God sent His Holy Spirit to his disciples fifty days after his resurrection. The disciples were gathered together in a room when suddenly there was a rush of wind, and they saw a flaming fire above each other's heads and they were filled with the Holy Spirit (see Acts 2: 2–4).

Saints' Days.   There are many days in the Christian calendar when particular saints (men and women) are remembered for the special contribution they made to the faith. Perhaps you could make a book about some of the saints. (see why St George, St Patrick or St Andrew are remembered today on pp. 230–3.)

Other Christian Denominations

Roman Catholics

The first disciples did as Jesus commanded them and began to spread the message of Christianity throughout the world. Peter (one of Jesus' disciples) was chosen as the first Bishop of Rome and became known as 'Papa' or Father, i.e. the first Pope. As head of the Roman Catholic Church, the Pope today resides in the Vatican in Rome, Italy. He is responsible for the world-wide Catholic church, its laws and rules.   Today's Pope is called Pope John Paul II, although he was born Karol Wojtyla.

Roman Catholics believe in one God and that Jesus Christ is His Son. They attend their parish church each Sunday where Mass or a reminder of the Last Supper is celebrated. Roman Catholics believe that the special bread, called the Host, and the wine become the actual body and blood of Jesus at their communion service.

After careful study and preparation classes, children of about 6 or 7 years old are allowed to make their first communion. They wear special clothes for this event and sometimes have a party afterwards.

The rosary is a set of beads, used as an aid to prayer. The Lord's Prayer is said, and special prayers to Mary, Jesus' mother, are made.

Eastern Orthodox Christians

The early Christian leaders in different countries were called 'Bishops'. They met to discuss various matters relating to church life and the Christian faith. However, in 1054, the Bishop of Rome and the Bishop of Constantinople became involved in a fearful struggle for power, which led to a split in the early church. The followers of the Bishop of Rome became known as Roman Catholics and the followers of the Bishop of Constantinople became known as Orthodox Christians. 'Orthodox' means 'right belief'.

Many Orthodox Christians live and worship in Greece, Cyprus, Russia, Yugoslavia, America and Britain today. Like all Christians, Orthodox Christians believe in one God, and that Jesus Christ is His Son; like the Catholics, they give Mary, Jesus' mother, a very special place in their worship.

Icons, or religious pictures, in the church are kissed by the worshippers before the Sunday service. The sign of the cross is made on entering the church, and each member of the congregation lights a candle. Incense is burnt, as a symbol of the prayers rising to God. Like the Roman Catholics, at Holy Communion, Orthodox Christians believe that the bread and wine become Christ's body and blood.

Every Orthodox baby is given the name of one of the saints, or Christ Himself, or Mary, the mother of Jesus, at a special baptismal service. The baby is put into water mixed with oil, three times, in the name of the Father, the Son and the Holy Spirit. Name days are very important in the Orthodox Church, and everyone makes a special effort to attend the church on their particular day.

The Protestant Reformation

The early church was to split again many times. It began in the early sixteenth century with a German priest called Martin Luther. He complained to the Pope that all the rules and regulations that had grown up around worship often prevented ordinary men and women from coming close to God.

This was the beginning of the Protestant movement. The Lutheran Church became important in Germany, Scandinavia and later America. The Anglican Church (or Church of England) is a Protestant Church and spread throughout the world. The Calvinist Church (named after John Calvin) 'laid the foundations of the Church of Scotland and other Presbyterian Churches' (Ward, 1973, p. 15). Basically, this early Protestant movement attempted to return to the teachings of the early church as revealed in the Bible. The reformers abolished many holy days, to give more importance to Christmas, Easter, Pentecost and Sunday worship. They emphasized the importance of baptism and Holy Communion.

Congregational Church

Although the Church of England had separated from Rome, many people in England still felt that the reforms had not gone far enough and that the established church was very corrupt. The Separatist Movement began as early as 1550 and gained momentum under the leadership of Robert Browne. Their central belief was that the local congregation formed the body of the church, with Jesus Christ as the head. They believed that where two or three were gathered together in His name, Christ was and is among them.

Each local congregation today chooses its own minister. No special dress is worn by the minister, although a black gown is usual for Sunday worship. Deacons are appointed from among the church members to run the church and to help with all matters financial and spiritual.

Baptist Church

Like the Congregationalists, the group calling themselves Baptists (in the early seventeenth century) were persecuted in England and fled to Holland. They differed from the Congregationalists in that they believed strictly in adult baptism, as depicted in the New Testament. Just as Jesus was baptized at the beginning of his ministry, Baptists believe that a person can only be baptized when he or she is ready to make his/her own promises to God for himself/herself. Baptists are completely submerged under water at the special baptismal service, as a sign of dying to sin and rising to a new way of life.

John Smyth, one of the exiles, was the first leader of this new movement in Holland in 1609. Many of his followers returned to London in approximately 1612 to set up Baptist churches and soon the movement grew all over the world.

Communion today in the Baptist Church is open to all who 'love the Lord Jesus Christ', and not just those who have been baptized. 'The Churches are gathered in local unions which belong in turn to the Baptist Union, meeting in annual assembly under an elected president' (Ward, 1973, p. 38).

Methodists

John Wesley was an Anglican clergyman, who did not set out to break with the Anglican Church. But, disillusioned by what he saw in the established churches, in the early eighteenth century he set about bringing 'the church' to the ordinary people by preaching in the open air. His message was the need for a personal faith and for conversion to a new way of life or 'method' for living, i.e. disciplined prayer life, reading the Bible and practising Christianity.

However, the break came about gradually, with John Wesley conducting the ordination of deacons and priests to preach in America; 'in 1784 the people called Methodists were recognized by Law (Ward, 1973, p. 41). After his death in 1791 the Methodists broke away from the Church of England, and Methodism soon spread throughout the world through the appointment of overseas missionaries.

The message today is much the same as for other Christians; namely, recognition of personal sin, a desire to be saved, a personal faith in Jesus Christ and evidence of a reformed way of life. Methodist services are more free than Anglican services today. There is more emphasis on hymn singing and extempore prayer.

The Salvation Army

William Booth, himself a Methodist minister, was the founder of the Salvation Army in 1865. He found Methodism too constricting, so founded a new movement, first called the East London Christian Mission but changed to the Salvation Army in 1878. William Booth decided to organize his volunteers along military lines to fight against evil and poverty. He appointed himself as the general, his fellow ministers became officers and the congregation became the soldiers, all wearing a uniform as a 'sign that they belonged to God's Army' (Blackwell, 1984, p. 5).

The brass band is an important feature of Salvation Army worship. The band helps to spread the Gospel message both at open air meetings and inside the Salvation Army citadels or halls.

The services are lead by a commanding officer or major who has been specially trained; many are women. The 'holiness meeting' or service does not follow a regular pattern. Sometimes the officers invite members of the congregation to give their testimony about following Jesus Christ, there is always a sermon, a Bible reading, joyful singing and a time of quiet reflective prayer. Other meetings are held such as the 'praise meeting' or the 'salvation meeting', and Salvation Army members hold music festivals and worship God through the use of drama.

Just like their founder, today Salvation Army members are at the forefront of the caring services, helping people who are the victims of poverty, earthquakes, wars and disasters.

Pentecostals

The Pentecostal movement has its roots in the early twentieth century. 'It grew out of a revival movement which took place in many parts of the world at the same time' (Pettenuzzo, 1986, p. 30).

Pentecostal conduct and style of worship are very much Bible-based, attempting to reflect the life-style of the early church and the teaching of Jesus. At Whitsun or Pentecost (fifty days after the resurrection of Jesus) Jesus' disciples were gathered together in one place for the Jewish festival of Shavout, when suddenly they heard a great noise like a rushing wind and saw little tongues of fire above each other's heads. This was the coming of the Holy Spirit which enabled the disciples to speak in foreign languages, so that people from different countries could understand what they were saying (see Acts 2). Pentecostals today pray for God's spirit to come upon them in the same way. They call this 'Baptism in the Spirit', which means being filled with the Holy Spirit and speaking in 'tongues', speech which has to be understood through an interpreter (Pettenuzzo, 1986, p. 30).

There are many Pentecostal churches all over the world today, and their number is still growing. It is a particularly popular form of worship in the West Indies, Africa, America and Britain.

No one can be 'born' a Pentecostal. Each church member has to confess his or her sins, and that Jesus Christ is Lord and Saviour and that they intend to live a 'new' life. Usually this takes place at an adult baptismal service, but children can be baptized too, so long as they are mature enough to understand the promises they are making. Baptism is by complete immersion in water, following the pattern of Jesus' own baptism in the River Jordan.

Music plays a very important part in Pentecostal worship. Singing, hand-clapping, instrument playing (especially the tambourine), rhythmic movement are all associated with Pentecostal worship. The congregation is often led by impressive choirs.

The leaders of the churches are called 'pastors', who can be men or women, and who are ordained ministers of the Pentecostal church. They are often assisted by deacons or elders. Evangelists or lay preachers also assist the pastor at services on Sundays, such as the 'divine worship service', the Lord's Supper, or at a 'healing service'. Afterwards, just as Jesus took a towel after the last supper with his disciples and began washing their feet, so too Pentecostals wash one another's feet after the Lord's Supper.

Resources

Books

(P) = Pupils
(T) = Teachers

BAILEY, J.R. *Founders, Prophets and Sacred Books* (Schofield and Sims, 1985) (T).
BAILEY, J.R. *Religious Buildings and Festivals* (Schofield and Sims, 1984) (T).
BAILEY, J.R. *Religious Leaders and Places of Pilgrimage Today* (Schofield and Sims, 1987) (T).
BATES, J. *Visiting a Methodist Church* (Lutterworth Educational, 1984) (T and P).
BLACKWELL, M. *Visiting a Salvation Army Citadel* (Lutterworth Educational, 1984) (T and P) (there are many more titles in this series).
COLLINSON, C. and MILLER, C. *Celebrations* (Edward Arnold, 1985), (T and P).
HACKEL, S. *The Orthodox Church* (Ward Lock Educational, 1971) (T).

HARRISON, S.W. and SHEPHERD, D. *A Christian Family in Britain* Exeter (Religious and Moral Education Press, 1986) (T and P).

HUGHES, R. *Nazareth* (Oxford University Press, 1984) (T and P) (this book forms part of a primary religious education course; there are more books in the series).

HUNT, D. *Jesus* (Oliver and Boyd, 1986) (P).

KILLINGRAY, M. and KILLINGRAY, J. *I Am an Anglican* (Franklin Watts, 1986) (P).

PETTENUZZO, B. *I Am a Pentecostal* (Franklin Watts, 1986) (P).

PETTENUZZO, B. *I Am a Roman Catholic* (Franklin Watts, 1985) (P).

ROUSSON, M. *I Am a Greek Orthodox* (Franklin Watts, 1985) (P).

THORLEY, S. *Christianity in Words and Pictures* (Religious and Moral Education Press, 1984) (T and P).

TRIGGS, T.D. *Founders of Religions* Hore (Wayland, 1981) (P).

WARD, M. *Protestant Christian Churches* (Ward Lock Educational, 1970).

Good News Bible (Bible Society, 1976).

The Lion Encyclopedia of the Bible, ten-part edition, Lion Publishing, 1980.

Addresses

Christian Education Movement,
2 Chester House,
Pages Lane,
London N10 1PR.